SUBMERGED IN THE
PROPHETIC

SUBMERGED IN THE PROPHETIC

A GUIDED EXPLORATION INTO THE DEPTHS OF PROPHECY

JOCELYN Y. BUCKLEY

SUBMERGED IN THE PROPHETIC
A GUIDED EXPLORATION INTO
THE DEPTHS OF PROPHECY

iUniverse books may be ordered through booksellers or by contacting:

iUniverse LLC
1663 Liberty Drive
Bloomington, IN 47403
www.iuniverse.com
1-800-Authors (1-800-288-4677)

Because of the dynamic nature of the Internet, any web addresses or links contained in this book may have changed since publication and may no longer be valid. The views expressed in this work are solely those of the author and do not necessarily reflect the views of the publisher, and the publisher hereby disclaims any responsibility for them.

Any people depicted in stock imagery provided by Thinkstock are models, and such images are being used for illustrative purposes only. Certain stock imagery © Thinkstock.

ISBN: 978-1-4917-4658-5 (sc)
ISBN: 978-1-4917-4659-2 (e)

Library of Congress Control Number: 2014916412

Printed in the United States of America.

iUniverse rev. date: 09/19/2014

To my mom, Annie Coleman, a kingdom warrior who has captured the heart of God. The strength, courage, and grace I've seen demonstrated through her has shaped me into the woman I am today. Thank you. I love you, Momma.

CONTENTS

ACKNOWLEDGMENTS

I am eternally grateful to God for inspiring me to write this book. I did not have an outline, scattered notes, or a written journal. God spoke clearly as I sat and listened. Thank you, God, for downloading into my spirit the information shared in this book from cover to cover.

My pastors, Bishop David C. Cooper and Co-Pastor Nina Cooper, have nurtured me for nearly twenty years throughout my own prophetic walk. Thank you for encouraging me along the journey.

Evangelist Shavon Sellers (Shavon Sellers Ministries), my mentor, inspired a group of women in the Empowering Moments Mentoring Program to reach their full potential. Thank you for pouring into us wisdom and knowledge that will help in our spiritual, professional, and personal development.

God has allowed me to be mentored by extraordinary and powerful men and women of God throughout the years. They have imparted wisdom and knowledge into my life regarding prophetic operations that have been instrumental in the development of my prophetic gift. Thank you tremendously.

My cousin, Deborah Harris, worked countless hours with me as we edited this book. She sacrificed her time spent with family, and I certainly want to acknowledge and thank her.

I am grateful to have worked with a group of talented and gifted individuals who exemplified professionalism and creativity during the development of this book. They are Diana Jackson (Web3D, LLC), graphics and web-site designer; Charles "Bazz" McClain (Basil Video Production), videographer; Donald Lipscomb, photographer; and the entire iUniverse publishing, editing, design, and production team.

INTRODUCTION

There is a time for everything, and a season for
every activity under the heavens.

—Ecclesiastes 3:1 NIV

There will be a time and a season in your prophetic walk
when God will take you through a place called isolation
because He wants you to see Him in all things. God
will take you through a place called rejection because He
wants you to realize that He accepts you as you are. He
will take you through a place called ridicule because He
wants you to see yourself as He sees you. God will take
you through so your prophetic utterance will be wrapped
in His Spirit and not covered in flesh.

The times and seasons of "going through" give birth
to the prophetic in you. You're positioned for purpose and
anointed for the assignment. As the Lord guides your steps
and moves you closer to that prophetic place in Him, your
perception of each test, trial, challenge, and circumstance
will change because your faith has increased.

Wherever you are in your prophetic journey, the Lord will find you there. If He finds you in the place of conflict, He'll send a resolution. If He finds you in the place of confusion, He'll send His peace. If He finds you in the place of chaos, He'll send order. If He finds you in the place of fear, He'll add faith. God will find you because He planted you. He will meet you wherever you are emotionally, spiritually, and physically, "Till we all come in the unity of the faith, and of the knowledge of the Son of God, unto a perfect man, unto the measure of the stature of the fullness of Christ" (Ephesians 4:13).

Submerged in the Prophetic will navigate you along your journey as a carrier of His word and a vessel for His spiritual gifts. As you walk through each chapter, I pray that your prophetic eyes will be opened and your heart will be enlightened in all wisdom, knowledge, and understanding by the Spirit of God who dwells within you. May the Lord leave an imprint on your heart, mind, soul, and spirit that will stir up the gifts in you and cause a shift in the heavens that will shake the earth into alignment at the sound of your prophetic utterance.

CHAPTER 1
GROWING UP BAPTIST

— ••• —

SAVED AND BAPTIST

Growing up Baptist was not an experience; it was a lifestyle. I remember waking up early Sunday mornings to the rhythmic melody of my mom's singing and the sweet aroma and crackling sound of bacon frying in the kitchen. The church we attended was right next door to our house, so I was expected to be there as soon as the doors opened. It was the neighborhood sanctuary, and nearly everyone in the neighborhood took his or her routine, Sunday-morning stroll to the little red-and-white church-house on the corner.

My experience at Mount Bethel (Missionary) Baptist Church was that of intrigue and excitement. Sundays were the days when families got together and ate from the Master's table. I remember the church mothers praising God in the corner with an intentional and deliberate hand clap or a sudden shout of "Amen!" or "Thank you, Jesus!"

I remember the deacons opening in prayer with songs like "Long as I Live and Trouble Rise" or "Father, I Stretch My Hand to Thee." We had no drummer, guitarist, or organist, only the harmonious melody created from within our hearts. The pastor preached with such jubilation that I waited in anticipation for the end of the sermon when the pastor's profound proclamations reverberated throughout the entire church. The church mothers and deacons yelled in agreement, and the congregants were on the edge of their seats.

During those days, we had no children's church. This meant we had to submit not only to our parents but also to the ushers. We dared not chew gum, talk, or even laugh in church, but it was hard not to burst out in occasional laughter from the silly things we created as children. Parents would bring switches to church and rest them beside us on the pew. For those who are unfamiliar with this early form of corporal punishment, these switches were thin, flexible branches (without leaves) taken from a small tree or bush in our yards. Our parents would swat our legs with those switches if we misbehaved as a reminder to behave properly in church. Those switches seated next to us spoke louder than the sermon.

I never experienced being slain in the Spirit or falling under the power of God, but I will never forget overhearing a conversation between my mom and aunt.

My cousin had apparently visited a "holiness" church with her friend, and my aunt was concerned because her daughter appeared to be "out of it" for some time. Isn't it interesting how folks tend to demonize that which they don't understand? Since then, my cousin has been a powerful, Spirit-filled intercessor and teacher. My mom and aunt are also Spirit-filled and mighty prayer warriors on fire for God. So I guess we're all under God's possession. My mom, aunt, and cousin are still faithful members of the same traditional Baptist churches they attended during my childhood.

As a child, I knew the mechanics of church but very little about the power of God that moved the mechanics. The Word of God says, "My people are destroyed for lack of knowledge: because thou has rejected knowledge, I will also reject thee, that thou shalt be no priest to me: seeing thou hast forgotten the law of thy God, I will also forget thy children" (Hosea 4:6).

Although I attended church regularly, I had little knowledge as it relates to the "full" gospel. I was only fed what someone else felt I could digest. I was taught the history of Jesus but failed to know the mystery of Christ.

Nevertheless, I was saved in that little Baptist church on the corner. I remember the moment of my salvation as though it were yesterday. As I knelt in prayer during a five-day revival, God revealed to me a vision of Jesus on the cross. In the vision, I stood among the crowd looking up at Him, crying "Jesus, Jesus save me!" Immediately, God spoke to me in an audible voice, "You are saved," and at that moment, my life changed.

You can receive the gift of salvation in a Baptist church. God can call you into the fivefold ministry of the apostle, prophet, evangelist, pastor, or teacher in a Baptist church. You can be healed and delivered in a Baptist church. You can receive the infilling of the Holy Spirit in a Baptist church. God looks at the heart and is not biased by a particular denomination. Just as He calls the pastor to shepherd the church, He can call an apostle to establish it. Just as He calls the evangelist to win souls with His *logos* (written) Word, He can also call a prophet to minister to souls with the *rhema* (revelatory) Word "because God does not show partiality" (Romans 2:11 ISV).

Chosen before Birth

"Before I formed thee in the belly I knew thee; and before thou camest forth out of the womb I sanctified thee, and I ordained thee a prophet unto the nations" (Jeremiah 1:5).

Before Jeremiah was formed in his mother's womb, God knew him and ordained him a prophet. God also knew you as spirit before you were formed in your mother's womb or were a thought in the mind of your parents. In fact, you are actually a thought from God, manifested. You were first created in God's imagination (image) and formed, or made manifest, through His prophetic proclamation. God has endowed every Spirit-filled believer with the supernatural ability to prophetically form and speak life into those who view their world as seemingly void and formless. As God's mouthpiece, you represent Him to the world through prophetic utterances and the operation of spiritual gifts. As God's mouthpiece, you are called to proclaim the heart and mind of Christ in the earth realm to the believer, unbeliever, skeptic, atheist, and traditionalist.

"Being confident of this very thing, that he which hath begun a good work in you will perform it until the day of Jesus Christ" (Philippians 1:6). It doesn't matter if you're Baptist, Methodist, Catholic, Presbyterian, Pentecostal, or nondenominational; God will complete His good work in you. It doesn't matter if you were baptized in Jesus' name or in the name of the Father, Son, and Holy Ghost; God will complete His good work in you. It doesn't even matter if you were sprinkled or submerged; God will complete His good work in you. Jesus responded to the thief on the cross, "Verily I say unto thee, To day shalt thou be with me in paradise"

(Luke 23:43). The thief had not been baptized in anyone's name.

You are the called and chosen of God, and His gifts and callings are without repentance. The

> "*The Kingdom of God does not discriminate.*

Lord anoints whom He appoints, and nothing can stop the oil from flowing through you. Do not waste His anointing oil discussing matters of denominationalism. The kingdom of God does not discriminate. The time to fulfill God's prophetic purpose in the earth is now. "For the earnest expectation of the creature waiteth for the manifestation of the sons of God" (Romans 8:19).

Chapter 2

PROPHETIC SEASONS

---•◦•---

It is God who alters the times and seasons, and he removes kings and promotes kings. He gives wisdom to the wise and knowledge to the discerning.

—Daniel 2:21 ISV

Discerning the Times

Nothing can reverse or stop the call of God on your life. Whether it is fulfilled through you or generations to follow, God's Word will accomplish its mission. "So shall my word be that goeth forth out of my mouth: it shall not return unto me void, but it shall accomplish that which I please, and it shall prosper in the thing whereto I sent it" (Isaiah 55:11). If God has to extend time to complete His assignment through you, He will. Ask Hezekiah.

Turn again, and tell Hezekiah the captain of my people, Thus saith the LORD, the God of David thy

father, I have heard thy prayer, I have seen thy tears:
behold, I will heal thee: on the third day thou shalt
go up unto the house of the LORD. And I will add
unto thy days fifteen years; and I will deliver thee
and this city out of the hand of the king of Assyria;
and I will defend this city for mine own sake, and
for my servant David's sake. And Isaiah said, Take
a lump of figs. And they took and laid it on the
boil, and he recovered. (2 Kings 20:5–7)

As budding prophetic men and women who are called
to speak the oracles of God in the earth, the mistake comes
when we move before His *kairos* (perfect) timing. We see
things in the "now" and have not learned to distinguish
prophetic seasons. As the seasons are in a particular order
in the natural, so they are in the spiritual. "The spiritual
did not come first, but the natural, and after that the
spiritual" (1 Corinthians 15:46 NIV). In the natural, a
tree grows and develops before producing fruit.

It is imperative to understand prophetic seasons, not
only in our lives but also in the lives of those who are
assigned to us. The call of God is not an indication to
uproot and plant one's self in a church or ministry that
embraces the prophetic. As a practical illustration, my
grandmother knew when to gather collard greens from her
garden. Although it was their harvest season, she did not

pick them until days before the first frost. It may be your season but not your time. As prophetic men and women of God, we must discern the times—even our own.

THE ISSACHAR ANOINTING

"And the children of Issachar, which were men that had understanding of the times, to know what Israel ought to do; the heads of them were two hundred; and all their brethren were at their commandment" (1 Chronicles 12:32).

The word *understanding* in Hebrew is the word *biynah*, which corresponds to knowledge and wisdom. It comes from a root verb, *biyn*, which means to separate something mentally (or distinguish), to attend, consider, discern, skillfully teach, think, or deal wisely.[1] In other words, understanding, in the context of this particular passage, means to dig deep into the facts, break them down, and analyze their true meaning.

Two hundred leaders of the tribe of Issachar are highlighted in the Word of God as men who understood public affairs, the mood of the nation, and the propensities of current events. These men submitted to King Saul, a descendant from the tribe of Benjamin, because they knew it was not time for David to become their ruler. It was obvious that King Saul had been an evil king, and there was no established dynasty to keep the kingship within his tribe.

During King Saul's reign, David had emerged as a real leader because of his integrity, character, and ability. After the death of King Saul, all of the tribes of Issachar declared David as their new king.[2] During those turbulent times, the events were God-ordained and led up to the fulfillment of prophecy. The ultimate Ruler—the Messiah, Jesus Christ—would come from the tribe of Judah. "The scepter will not depart from Judah, nor the ruler's staff from between his feet, until he to whom it belongs shall come and the obedience of the nations shall be his" (Genesis 49:10 NIV).

Before we make a decision that could result in the delay of our prophetic growth, we must first use our God-given intelligence and wisdom to understand the times. The Word of God declares, "The beginning of wisdom is this: Get wisdom. Though it cost all you have, get understanding" (Proverbs 4:7 NIV). Don't step out of your garden, your church, too soon. Even though it is your season, it may not be your time. In God's perfect time, the sons of Issachar will rise up in your region and cause a shift in leadership to take place, launching you into the next prophetic dimension in Him.

The Lord is developing you into a powerful prophetic voice and influential leader in your area. The ability to correctly analyze the current political climate is a component of effective leadership. Lord, give us the wisdom, knowledge, intelligence, and insight to understand the current times and to make strategic moves that will change the political and prophetic climate of this generation.

PURGED, PRUNED, AND PREPARED

Our temple must be purged, pruned, and prepared for our kingdom assignment, which starts on our

> "*Prophecy is birthed through prayer.*

knees in prayer. During prayer, we surrender our will and submit to His will. Jesus said to His Father, "Nevertheless not my will, but thine, be done" (Luke 22:42). Many want to prophesy, but so few are willing to pray. Prophecy is birthed through prayer.

> And he cometh unto the disciples, and findeth them asleep, and saith unto Peter, What, could ye not watch with me one hour? Watch and pray, that ye enter not into temptation: the spirit indeed is willing, but the flesh is weak. (Matthew 26:40–41)

There were nights I wept in travail for the church. During this season of my prophetic walk, God was actually changing me, molding me, building character in me, teaching me how to hear His voice, and testing me to see if I could be trusted with His secrets. I stopped battling with my own consciousness and accepted my placement. Although I was placed there, I knew my purpose was not boxed inside of four walls. As I stayed in place, my prophetic training developed exponentially—in a traditional church.

Chapter 3

YOUR PROPHETIC WALK

When the LORD was about to take Elijah up to heaven in a whirlwind, Elijah and Elisha were on their way from Gilgal. Elijah said to Elisha, "Stay here; the LORD has sent me to Bethel." But Elisha said, "As surely as the LORD lives and as you live, I will not leave you." So they went down to Bethel ... Then Elijah said to him, "Stay here, Elisha; the LORD has sent me to Jericho." And he replied, "As surely as the LORD lives and as you live, I will not leave you." So they went to Jericho ... Then Elijah said to him, "Stay here; the LORD has sent me to the Jordan." And he replied, "As surely as the LORD lives and as you live, I will not leave you." So the two of them walked on.

—2 Kings 2:1–6 NIV

HEALING AT GILGAL

You must start in Gilgal before you journey into Jordan. Gilgal means "rolling" or "roll away."[1]

> And after the whole nation had been circumcised, they remained where they were in camp until they were healed. Then the LORD said to Joshua, "Today I have rolled away the reproach of Egypt from you." So the place has been called Gilgal to this day. (Joshua 5:8–9 NIV)

The stone of a painful past and the shame of a belligerent bondage are rolled away at Gilgal, the place where God separates you for the work of the kingdom, the place of separation from all of the taunts and lies that whisper in your ear, saying, "You will never get to your promised land," or "You will never amount to anything." Gilgal draws you closer to God through the circumstances that enter into your experience. It is the first place you must decide to either stay with your spiritual covering or walk away. Will you affirm, as Elisha, "As surely as the Lord lives and as you live, I will not leave you?"

Gilgal is your initial training ground in the School of the Prophets. Will it break you or make you? In the natural, there are classes deemed by students as weed-out classes, those first few classes taken within a particular major that are usually the most difficult. These classes challenge you and may cause you to question your academic path. Stay on the journey. Gilgal is not meant to break you but to make you.

WORSHIP AT BETHEL

Your own desires and self-will were sacrificed during the altar experience of your prophetic journey at Gilgal so you could enter into Bethel healed, whole, and completely surrendered to God's will for your life. It was Jacob who first called this place Bethel because this is where he met the Lord.

> When Jacob awoke from his sleep, he thought, "Surely the LORD is in this place, and I was not aware of it." He was afraid and said, "How awesome is this place! This is none other than the house of God; this is the gate of heaven." Early the next morning Jacob took the stone he had placed under his head and set it up as a pillar and poured oil on top of it. He called that place Bethel, though the city used to be called Luz. (Genesis 28:16–19 NIV)

Bethel in Greek means "House of El" or "House of God."[2] Jacob had been in the presence of the Lord at the "gate of heaven" in the place he called Bethel. The anointing of God was there, which was symbolized by his setting up a stone as a pillar and "pour[ing] oil on top of it" as an altar for God. As we enter into His presence at Bethel, God will open the "gate of heaven" and begin to pour out fresh revelation for His people. Bethel is a place of worship, and worship propels us into the realm of prophecy.

> *"Worship propels us into the realm of prophecy.*

> But now bring me a minstrel. And it came to pass, when the minstrel played, that the hand of the LORD came upon him [Elisha]. And he said, Thus saith the LORD, Make this valley full of ditches. For thus saith the LORD, Ye shall not see wind, neither shall ye see rain; yet that valley shall be filled with water, that ye may drink, both ye, and your cattle, and your beasts. (2 Kings 3:15–17)

The sound of worship helped usher Elisha into a prophetic realm, and he began to prophesy the Word of the Lord.

Our desire at Bethel should be for God's presence to gently rest upon our hearts. Bethel is the place of intimacy with our Father, close enough to hear His whisper. At Bethel, our prophetic flow is synchronized with His heartbeat. At Bethel, we are standing at the gate of an open heaven receiving fresh revelation from the throne room of God. As we receive this prophetic stream, we have a responsibility to pour it onto God's people as they become saturated in the overflow. Nothing else matters at Bethel but God.

Victory at Jericho

Now Jericho was straitly shut up because of the children of Israel: none went out, and none came in. And the LORD said unto Joshua, See, I have given into thine hand Jericho, and the king thereof, and the mighty men of valour. And ye shall compass the city, all ye men of war, and go round about the city once. Thus shalt thou do six days. And seven priests shall bear before the ark seven trumpets of rams' horns: and the seventh day ye shall compass the city seven times, and the priests shall blow with the trumpets. And it shall come to pass, that when they make a long blast with the ram's horn, and when ye hear the sound of the trumpet, all the people shall shout with a great shout; and the wall of the city shall fall down flat, and the people shall ascend up every man straight before him. (Joshua 6:1–5)

At Jericho, Elijah and Elisha are nearing the end of their prophetic journey together. Historically, Jericho

> " *The walls obey the prophetic sound.*

is the place of the Israelites' first battle in the Promised Land. The Israelites were able to take the city because they followed the instructions their leader, Joshua, received from God. Jericho is a place where you come to the realization that your spiritual covering carries the instructions of the Lord. When the instructions are followed, the walls that are hindering your prophetic progress will collapse. Also the walls of religion, racism, social injustice, and financial and economic struggles will fall as you obey God at Jericho. The walls surrounding your heart, which may have been broken because of the enemy's lies concerning your destiny, will tumble as you obey the voice of the Lord. The prophetic war cry coming through you will break the wall of generational curses that may have plagued your family for years. The walls obey the prophetic sound, and only you can produce the sound that will shatter the strongholds (walls) in your life.

Jericho is a place of authentic praise. Even the devil can praise God and make it look real. In fact, he was the praise and worship leader before being cast out of heaven because he thought he should be the one worshipped rather than the worshipper. This act of treason cost him everything (Ezekiel 28:12–19; Isaiah 14:12; Luke 10:18; Revelation 12:3–9). As you approach your "seventh day," take the city with authentic praise. When praise goes up, the walls come down.

Jericho is located in the Jordan valley, and valleys are defined as areas of low land between hills or mountains.[3] All of us will encounter a valley season in our prophetic walk. None of us are exempt from Jericho. Realize that in those seasons, Jordan is just up the hill. Exercise your faith, find the courage to reach within yourself, and climb. The Spirit of God will provide the extra lift needed to help you reach the top. Jericho demonstrates your prophetic walk in faith. You are well able to continue the journey, so march.

CROSSING JORDAN

And Elijah took his mantle, and wrapped it together, and smote the waters, and they were divided hither and thither, so that they two went over on dry ground. And it came to pass, when they were gone over, that Elijah said unto Elisha, Ask what I shall do for thee, before I be taken away from thee. And Elisha said, I pray thee, let a double portion of thy spirit be upon me. And he said, Thou hast asked a hard thing: nevertheless, if thou see me when I am taken from thee, it shall be so unto thee; but if not, it shall not be so. And it came to pass, as they still went on, and talked, that, behold, there appeared a chariot of fire, and horses of fire, and parted them both asunder; and Elijah went up by a whirlwind into heaven. (2 Kings 2:8–11)

At Jordan, the prophetic mantle, or cloak, that rested upon Elijah was transferred to his protégé, Elisha. After this divine transfer, Elisha received a "double portion" of Elijah's anointing, and Elijah was translated into heaven by a whirlwind. Jordan is a place of miracles, signs, and wonders. It is a place where God will divide the waters in order for His people to reach the fulfillment of His promises. After the prophetic mantle is released into the protégé's life, the anointing will speak for itself.

And he took the mantle of Elijah that fell from him, and smote the waters, and said, "Where is the LORD God of Elijah?" And when he also had smitten the waters, they parted hither and thither: and Elisha went over. (2 Kings 2:14)

The prophetic anointing will speak to the skeptics, cynics, doubters, atheists, agnostics, and any other unbelievers that may be hanging around mocking the mantle God has placed on your life. It wasn't until the onlookers saw Elisha part the waters that they said to one another, "'The spirit of Elijah doth rest on Elisha.' And they came to meet him, and bowed themselves to the ground before him" (2 Kings 2:15). God will speak to your onlookers through the gifts He has placed within you, and they will begin to honor the Gifter within you.

Jordan is first mentioned in Genesis 13. The Law of First Mention is the principle that requires one to go to that portion of the Scriptures where a particular word or doctrine is mentioned for the first time and study the first occurrence in order to get the fundamental inherent meaning of that word or doctrine.[4] The "first mention" of the word *Jordan* has to do with matters of separation, as this is the place where Lot separated from Abram.

And Lot lifted up his eyes, and beheld all the plain of Jordan, that it was well watered everywhere, before the LORD destroyed Sodom and Gomorrah, even as the garden of the LORD, like the land of Egypt, as thou comest unto Zoar. Then Lot chose him all the plain of Jordan; and Lot journeyed east: and they separated themselves the one from the other. Abram dwelled in the land of Canaan, and Lot dwelled in the cities of the plain, and pitched his tent toward Sodom. (Genesis 13:10–12)

There will come a time in your prophetic walk when a decision must be made regarding your attachments. Attachments are not assignments. Those assigned to you will stick with you during the hard places of your journey. Those assigned to you are the ones who will encourage you to keep climbing during your Jericho (valley) experiences. They are the motivators in your life. They are the ones who will pray you through. Those assigned to you are in relationship with you and desire to watch you grow spiritually. The attachments, however, will slip away and leave during the most difficult seasons of your walk. Make the right decision at Jordan. Stay connected to your assignments and detach from the attachments.

Elijah's ascension to heaven occurred at the Jordan, resulting in his separation from Elisha and the disciples of the prophet from the School of the Prophets that Elijah had founded. Notice it wasn't Elisha who separated from his leader; it was Elijah who separated from his student. Elijah's ascension (separation) took place not for his own sake but for those who were left behind. God allowed it to happen this way so that Elijah's students from the School of the Prophets would become firmly established in their calling by the miraculous glorification of their leader than by his words, teaching, or his admonitions. God allowed Elijah's translation to occur in this manner so his students would continue in their calling without fear.[5]

The Hebrew meaning of the name Jordan is "the descender." It is connected with the Hebrew verb *yarad*, which means "to come or go down."[6] Jordan is the place in us that has to "descend" so His spirit can ascend through us. Your Jordan may be fear, but replace it with faith. Your Jordan may be low-self esteem, but replace it with confidence. Your Jordan may be hurt, but replace it with forgiveness. Your Jordan may be anger, but replace it with love. Whatever Jordan is keeping you from possessing, ask the Lord to consume it completely so you can cross over it and possess His prophetic promises. "For ye shall pass over Jordan to go in to possess the land which the LORD your God giveth you, and ye shall possess it, and dwell therein" (Deuteronomy 11:31).

Your prophetic walk and encounters through Gilgal, Bethel, Jericho, and Jordan are necessary for your prophetic development and spiritual growth. Keep pressing, and resolve not to remain motionless. Be encouraged, and know the Lord is with you and that His Spirit is carrying you.

I am reminded of a beautiful poem, "Footprints in the Sand," written by Mary Stevenson in 1936.[7] The poet shares a dream of walking along the beach with the Lord. In some scenes she only noticed one set of footprints during the most difficult times in her life. The poet then asked the Lord, "Why, when I needed you most, have you not been there for me?" The Lord replied, "The years when you have seen only one set of footprints, my child, is when I carried you."

Continue along your journey because God is waiting to greet you face-to-face at your final resting place—heaven. There you will hear Him say, "This is my son/daughter, in whom I am well pleased."

Chapter 4

A SEED PLANTED

—●—

I [Paul] have planted, Apollos watered; but God gave the increase.

—1 Corinthians 3:6

Planted to Serve

You have been planted to minister. *Minister* in Greek is the word *diakonos*, which means:

> One who executes the commands of another, especially of a master; a servant, attendant, or minister; servant of a king; a deacon who one, by virtue of the office assigned to him by the church, cares for the poor and has charge of and distributes the money collected for their use; a waiter, one who serves food and drink.[1]

We must realize that our ultimate purpose is to minister or serve. Until we humble ourselves in the presence of God and to those whom He has entrusted us to serve, the release into our ultimate purpose will be delayed. Your purpose has very little to do with where you're planted, your position, or your title. Your purpose has more to do with your resulting transformation. Bloom where you are planted.

Prepare the Ground

God has placed His seed in you because He trusts the ground (your spirit) in which the seed has been planted. Having grown up in southern Mississippi, I understand the importance of properly tilled and fertilized ground before planting any kind of seed. Your ground must be fertilized with the Word of God continuously in order for a harvest to produce from the seed planted. Therefore, there are some actions you must take in order for His prophetic promises to be birthed within you. It is necessary that you till, fertilize, water, and nurture your ground before, during, and after the planting process. The Word of God gives us a beautiful illustration in the parable of the sower, which highlights the importance of having the right ground to plant the seed in to ensure its growth and an abundant harvest.

And he spake many things unto them in parables, saying, Behold, a sower went forth to sow; And when he sowed, some seeds fell by the way side, and the fowls came and devoured them up: Some fell upon stony places, where they had not much earth: and forthwith they sprung up, because they had no deepness of earth: And when the sun was up, they were scorched; and because they had no root, they withered away. And some fell among thorns; and the thorns sprung up, and choked them: But other fell into good ground, and brought forth fruit, some an hundredfold, some sixtyfold, some thirtyfold. Who hath ears to hear, let him hear. (Matthew 13:3–9)

Fertilize your ground with the Word of God, water your ground in worship, and nurture your ground in prayer so that when God's sows His seed in you, it will fall on good ground and bring forth much fruit. You determine your harvest (return) by carefully tending your ground.

THE HIDDEN SEED

When God plants the prophetic seed (word) into your ground (spirit), there has to be time for the seed to set and form. The seed establishes strong roots and matures and begins to grow beyond the ground as a result of the consistent watering of the Word of God. There is the seed. There is time. Then there is the harvest. "While the earth remaineth, seedtime and harvest, and cold and heat, and summer and winter, and day and night shall not cease" (Genesis 8:22).

While the seed is hidden, this is the time for you to discover who you truly are—a process that never really ends. This is the time for you to realize that there is potential, power, and purpose in the seed. This is the time for you to build strength from within and break through the ground (mindset) of limitation and lack.

Once the seed is planted, your purpose begins the process of revealing itself to you and those around you, but it starts in that hidden place deep within your soul. Yes, it may feel as though you are alone in the dark, trampled upon and flooded by the issues of life and suffocated by the cares of this world, but you are growing. It may not feel like you're growing, but you are. There is life in the seed.

After the seed is planted, it doesn't discuss its discomfort with other seeds. My mom has a green thumb, and I remember one day asking her how was she able to keep her plants alive and thriving for so long. They were always green and flourishing. My mom answered, "Talk to them, and tell them how beautiful they are." That is powerful and still resonates within my spirit. Watch the words that are spoken over your seed. Discerning those who are called to help the seed to grow and flourish is very important in the realm of the prophetic. There are many wolves dressed in sheep's clothing sent by the devil himself to prey upon your vulnerabilities while you are growing, maturing, and becoming grounded and rooted in the faith.

> And many false prophets shall rise, and shall deceive many. And because iniquity shall abound, the love of many shall wax cold. But he that shall endure unto the end, the same shall be saved. And this gospel of the kingdom shall be preached in all the world for a witness unto all nations; and then shall the end come. (Matthew 24:11–14)

Be watchful who you allow to speak over your seed and what you allow to enter into your ground. Ask the Lord for the gift of discerning of spirits in order for you to judge righteously. Actually, and in many instances, simply using common sense to assess the character and integrity of others is all that is needed. The Word of God says, "Beware of false prophets, which come to you in sheep's clothing, but inwardly they are ravening wolves. Ye shall know them by their fruits. Do men gather grapes of thorns, or figs of thistles" (Matthew 7:15–16)? For those who are in your current circle, ask yourself, "What is their seed producing? Is it producing good fruit, rotten fruit, or no fruit?" The answer doesn't take discernment but simply an inventory of the fruit produced by a person's lifestyle.

And it came to pass, that, when Elisabeth heard the salutation of Mary, the babe leaped in her womb; and Elisabeth was filled with the Holy Ghost: And she spake out with a loud voice, and said, Blessed art thou among women, and blessed is the fruit of thy womb. And whence is this to me, that the mother of my Lord should come to me? For, lo, as soon as the voice of thy salutation sounded in mine ears, the babe leaped in my womb for joy. And blessed is she that believed: for there shall be a performance of those things which were told her from the Lord. (Luke 1:41–45)

The seed of David was hidden in Mary's womb. Mary, being enveloped in God's glory, was led by the Holy Spirit straight to Elizabeth who had been barren but was now in her sixth month of pregnancy with the supernatural seed of John the Baptist.

You are not alone on this prophetic journey. You may be the only one called into the office of the prophet in that little Baptist church on the corner, but you are not the only prophet. The Bible records that once Elizabeth heard the salutation of Mary, the babe leaped in Elizabeth's womb and she was filled with the Holy Ghost and spoke with a loud voice. In other words, she prophesied. Go, and run to your Elizabeth. Your Elizabeth will speak life to your seed. Your Elizabeth will confirm the Word of the Lord that was spoken into your life. The seed in your Elizabeth will bear witness with the seed in you.

STAY PLANTED

When the prophetic seed has been planted in your spirit by God, your first responsibility is to submit to the growing stages. I've never seen a seed uproot itself from the ground, as that is out of order with the law of nature. During the growing stages of processing and preparation, God is teaching you how to love as He loves. He's teaching you how to study to be quiet. He's teaching you how to depend on Him to supply all of your needs.

> But as touching brotherly love ye need not that I write unto you: for ye yourselves are taught of God to love one another. And indeed ye do it toward all the brethren which are in all Macedonia: but we beseech you, brethren, that ye increase more

31

and more; And that ye study to be quiet, and to do your own business, and to work with your own hands, as we commanded you; That ye may walk honestly toward them that are without, and that ye may have lack of nothing. (1 Thessalonians 4:9–12)

Do not become anxious. In fact, the Word of God says, "Be anxious for nothing, but in everything by prayer and supplication with thanksgiving let your requests be made known to God" (Philippians 4:6–7 NASB). During this time of teaching and training, learn the triggers that alert you to His voice; learn prophetic timing and order; and attune your hearing to distinguish the prophetic sound that penetrates a nation, region, state, city, and community and your church.

The prophetic is not dependent upon denominations, nor is it bound by borders, but prophecy has everything to do with the establishment of God's kingdom on Earth. "Thy kingdom come. Thy will be done *in earth*, as it is in heaven" (Matthew 6:10, emphasis added). Your ground must be stable so that when the tests come, the fruit of your works from the seed that was once planted in you will not be destroyed. Your steps have been ordered by God—stay planted.

THE SCAFFOLDING

In the natural realm, it could take months and even years to build a structure. The quality of the building dictates the time it takes to complete. The material used during the building process is crucial in determining the integrity of the building. As a student of the prophetic, it is imperative that you allow *the* master builder (God) to complete His work in you, which starts with a solid foundation, so when the building (your temple) is tested, it will stand.

> According to the grace of God which is given unto me, as a wise masterbuilder, I have laid the foundation, and another buildeth thereon. But let every man take heed how he buildeth thereupon. For other foundation can no man lay than that is laid, which is Jesus Christ. Now if any man build upon this foundation gold, silver, precious stones, wood, hay, stubble; Every man's work shall be made manifest: for the day shall declare it, because it shall be revealed by fire; and the fire shall try every man's work of what sort it is. If any man's work abide which he hath built thereupon, he shall receive a reward. If any man's work shall be burned, he shall suffer loss: but he himself shall be saved; yet so as by fire. (1 Corinthians 3:10–15)

When a building is constructed in the natural, there is often scaffolding to provide a safe place to work with safe access suitable for the work performed. However, scaffoldings are not part of the permanent structure or building. Realize during your prophetic journey that there will be scaffolding (people) God will place in your path to help you as He builds. Discern who serves as scaffolding in your life, those who are only assigned to be with you for the short term. If the scaffolding remains too long, it can actually be a hindrance to the building process. When the scaffolding leaves or is removed by God, let it go. Don't reach back for the scaffolding because it has actually served its purpose. Every so often you should take an inventory of the work (building) God is creating in you, and ask God to remove any excess material (scaffolding) that has already served its purpose.

Now It Shall Spring Forth

"Behold, I will do a new thing; now it shall spring forth; shall you not know it? I will even make a way in the wilderness, and rivers in the desert" (Isaiah 43:19).

God is doing a new thing in you. Many of you will experience a sudden shift into a new anointing. This new thing the Lord is doing in you will spring forth from you because the seed has been planted in good ground. The Word says that *now* it shall spring forth. Your *now* is sooner than you think. Your *now* has already manifested in the heavenly realm and is making its way into the earthly realm. Your *now* will dig deep into your ground and create rivers in the dry places. Your *now* will meet you where you are. Whether it is in a Baptist, Catholic, Methodist, Presbyterian, Pentecostal, or nondenominational church, your *now* will meet you there. When your *now* shows up, embrace it.

> "When your now shows up, embrace it.

Chapter 5

SPIRITUAL COVERING

———•‣•———

And I will give you pastors according to mine
heart, which shall feed you with knowledge and
understanding.

—Jeremiah 3:15

A Pastor's Heart

Pastors after God's own heart impart knowledge, wisdom,
and understanding to believers and nonbelievers. Pastors
after God's own heart are anointed to heal and not hurt,
to deliver truth and not deny it. Pastors after God's own
heart obey the Spirit of the Lord and not the flesh of men.
Pastors after God's own heart shepherd the sheep and dare
not suffocate them. True pastors follow the example Jesus
set on the earth. He said,

The Spirit of the Lord is upon me, because he
hath anointed me to preach the gospel to the poor;

he hath sent me to heal the brokenhearted, to preach deliverance to the captives, and recovering of sight to the blind, to set at liberty them that are bruised, To preach the acceptable year of the Lord. (Luke 4:18–19)

The release into ministry will come through your pastor as he or she obeys the voice of God. It will come in God's timing, and not your own. Your pastor is your spiritual covering. Therefore, do not attempt to step out and move in the things of God uncovered. It is better to be sent than to be among the many fallen ones who just went. Remember, God is not bound by time, because He is eternal. He is able to accelerate time or slow it down on your behalf. In fact, He can even restore it. Be patient. "And I will restore to you the years that the locust hath eaten, the cankerworm, and the caterpiller, and the palmerworm, my great army which I sent among you" (Joel 2:25).

Pastors cover us in prayer continuously. The pastor's covering is there to protect us during our maturing process. Shepherds (pastors) hurt when one sheep has gone astray and will leave everything to go after that one misguided sheep. As stated previously, the Word of God warns us to beware of the wolves that are dressed in sheep's clothing, and as children of God, who are still growing in the prophetic, we need help in discerning the true from the false. We need our pastors.

THEOLOGICAL HERITAGE

We need the old move of God to help usher us into the new move of God. We need our foundation on which to build. Our *theological heritage* should remind us of where the Lord has brought us. *Theological* is defined as "relating to the study of God and religion." *Heritage* is defined as "the art, buildings, traditions, and beliefs that a society considers important to its history and culture."[1] Our pastors not only impart wisdom, knowledge, and understanding about our theological heritage, but they also help transition us into the next wave of God's glory. The Word of God declares that we progress from glory to glory. "But we all, with open face beholding as in a glass the glory of the Lord, are changed into the same image from glory to glory, even as by the Spirit of the Lord" (2 Corinthians 3:18).

The theological heritage passed down from Eli to Samuel was crucial in shaping Samuel to become a great judge, prophet, and priest. We, too, need an Eli to help us distinguish the voice of God from the voice of man, the enemy, or our own consciousness. Eli helped Samuel discern God's voice.

Now Samuel did not yet know the LORD, neither was the word of the LORD yet revealed unto him. And the LORD called Samuel again the third time. And he arose and went to Eli, and said, Here am I; for thou didst call me. And Eli perceived that the LORD had called the child. Therefore Eli said unto Samuel, Go, lie down: and it shall be, if he call thee, that thou shalt say, Speak, LORD; for thy servant heareth. So Samuel went and lay down in his place. (1 Samuel 3:7–9)

Samuel mistakenly thought Eli was calling him. This is a great example of being close to your spiritual covering, not to the point of familiarity, yet spiritually connected where the voice of your pastor is the voice of the Lord in your ear. Eli perceived that it was the Lord calling Samuel and told Samuel not only what to do but also instructed him on what to say. "And the LORD came, and stood, and called as at other times, Samuel, Samuel. Then Samuel answered, Speak; for thy servant heareth" (1 Samuel 3:10).

As growing Samuels serving under our Elis, we need our spiritual father or mother to help us discern God's voice and direct us as to how to properly respond when He calls. There are many voices in the air, but only God's voice is The Voice. "My sheep hear my voice, and I know them and they follow me" (John 10:27).

CONSIDER MOSES

> And the LORD said unto Moses, Gather unto me
> seventy men of the elders of Israel, whom thou
> knowest to be the elders of the people, and officers
> over them; and bring them unto the tabernacle
> of the congregation, that they may stand there
> with thee. And I will come down and talk with
> thee there: and I will take of the spirit which is
> upon thee, and will put it upon them; and they
> shall bear the burden for the people with thee,
> That thou bear it not thyself alone. (Numbers
> 11:16–17)

Moses symbolizes the pastor's role in the modern-day
church. As he was commissioned to lead the children of
Israel out of Egypt, our pastor has also been commissioned
to lead us into our promised land. And not only do we
need our pastor, our pastor needs his staff: "Raise your
staff and stretch out your hand over the sea to divide the
water so that the Israelites can go through the sea on dry
ground" (Exodus 14:16 NIV).

We serve as an extension of our pastor's arms or as
the staff for our leader. As our pastor casts out his or her
God-given vision for the church, city, state, region, and/
or nation, he or she also raises up his or her staff. It is the

responsibility of the pastor's staff to "divide the water" and execute the vision. If we are not aligned with the pastor's God-given vision, it creates division among the staff that will eventually trickle into the congregation. In spite of the little inconveniences you may encounter as you follow your pastor, in spite of the fact that Pharaoh's army is chasing you, reminding you of your past bondage and enticing you to return to old habits, you must trust your pastor and know that he or she will lead you into your prophetic promises. Follow your pastor as your pastor follows Christ.

Hidden for a Purpose

"Do not despise these small beginnings, for the LORD rejoices to see the work begin, to see the plumb line in Zerubbabel's hand." (Zechariah 4:10a NLT).

Stay covered, and do not despise small beginnings. You are hidden for a purpose. God recognizes the value in you, and so does your pastor. A pearl is hidden in the shell of an oyster for a reason and a season. "Give not that which is holy unto the dogs, neither cast ye your pearls before swine, lest they trample them under their feet, and turn again and rend you" (Matthew 7:6).

Stepping out from under your covering prematurely can be detrimental to the prophetic voice God is refining in you. Hear and obey the counsel of God through your pastor. Pastors after God's own heart care for their sheep and want the best for them. They nurture their sheep. True shepherds pray for their sheep, but hirelings prey on the sheep. "But he that is an hireling, and not the shepherd, whose own the sheep are not, seeth the wolf coming, and leaveth the sheep, and fleeth: and the wolf catcheth them, and scattereth the sheep" (John 10:12).

> "*True shepherds pray for their sheep, but hirelings prey on the sheep.*

You may think your pastor is holding you back, but in reality he or she is protecting you from the wolves dressed in sheep's clothing that he or she sees lurking in the distance. When you are ready, the Lord will use your pastor to reveal and release you into ministry, and it will be done decently and in order.

THE COVERING OF ELI

> But Samuel ministered before the LORD, being a child, girded with a linen ephod. Moreover his mother made him a little coat, and brought it to him from year to year, when she came up with her husband to offer the yearly sacrifice. And Eli blessed Elkanah and his wife, and said, The LORD give thee seed of this woman for the loan which is lent to the LORD. And they went unto their own home. (1 Samuel 2:18–20)

Samuel served Eli faithfully from early childhood. Even though he saw the wickedness and disorder among Eli's sons, he remained under Eli's covering.

> Now the sons of Eli were sons of Belial; they knew not the LORD ... Now Eli was very old, and heard all that his sons did unto all Israel; and how they lay with the women that assembled at the door of the tabernacle of the congregation. And he said unto them, Why do ye such things? for I hear of your evil dealings by all this people. Nay, my sons; for it is no good report that I hear: ye make the LORD's people to transgress. If one man sin against another, the judge shall judge him: but if

a man sin against the LORD, who shall intreat for him? Notwithstanding they hearkened not unto the voice of their father, because the LORD would slay them. (1 Samuel 2:12, 22–25)

Even in the midst of witnessing the sins of Eli's sons, Samuel did not retreat from his responsibilities, nor is it written that he asked Eli to send him back to his mother. There is no record of Samuel complaining to Eli about the conditions that existed in the house of God. Samuel never wavered in his assignment because he knew his purpose. The Word of God says, "For he that wavereth is like a wave of the sea driven with the wind and tossed. For let not that man think that he shall receive anything of the Lord. A double-minded man is unstable in all his ways" (James 1:6–8). Samuel remained stable. In fact, the Bible records that "Samuel stayed in bed until morning, then got up and opened the doors of the Tabernacle as usual" (1 Samuel 3:15a NLT).

I can just see Samuel serving around the altar, making sure the sacrifice is ready, preparing the priestly garments, and opening the doors of the house of God. I can see modern-day Samuels serving their Elis, and not leaving his or her side. I can see little Samuels praying for their Elis, unlocking the doors of the church, making sure the pulpit area is presentable and the sanctuary is clean, greeting the people with a warm smile and escorting them to their seats. Yes, Samuel served with his whole heart. Samuel's passion propelled his purpose.

During his time of serving, Samuel studied his pastor. He gleaned from his spiritual father, Eli. Samuel needed Eli, and in turn, Eli needed Samuel to share the prophecy God had given Samuel concerning Eli's house:

> Then Eli called Samuel, and said, Samuel, my son. And he answered, Here am I. And he said, What is the thing that the LORD hath said unto thee? I pray thee hide it not from me: God do so to thee, and more also, if thou hide anything from me of all the things that he said unto thee. And Samuel told him every whit, and hid nothing from him. And he said, It is the LORD: let him do what seemeth him good. (1 Samuel 3:16–18)

Because of Samuel's obedience and faithfulness to God in serving Eli, the Word says, "And Samuel grew, and the LORD was with him, and did let none of his words fall to the ground" (1 Samuel 3:19).

In the fullness of time, the Lord ultimately used Eli to release Samuel into ministry. The Word also says that Samuel was "established" to be a prophet of the Lord. "And all Israel from Dan even to Beersheba knew that

Samuel was established to be a prophet of the LORD" (1 Samuel 3:20).

Not only was Eli instrumental in Samuel's release but also in establishing him in ministry. This tells me that one can be released but not properly established. If your pastor or spiritual covering does not properly release you, you may find it difficult to become established in ministry. Your foundation will be exposed, making you vulnerable, "tossed to and fro, and carried about with every wind of doctrine, by the sleight of men, and cunning craftiness, whereby they lie in wait to deceive" (Ephesians 4:14).

God's release and establishment comes through faithfully serving the man or woman of God that He has placed as your spiritual covering. Because of Samuel's faithfulness, none of his words fell to the ground, and he grew to become a judge, a prophet, and a priest. You never know the exact path God has for you, but serving those whom God has sent is the key that will unlock your prophetic destiny.

The Covering of Saul

After Samuel's release into ministry, he was eventually commissioned by God to anoint David as future king of Israel: "Then Samuel took the horn of oil, and anointed him in the midst of his brethren: and the Spirit of the

LORD came upon David from that day forward. So Samuel rose up, and went to Ramah" (1 Samuel 16:13).

However, even after David was anointed to become king, before he could fulfill his assignment, he had to submit to his spiritual covering, King Saul. Yes, the same king who became so blinded with jealousy and anger that he conspired to kill David. This same king, who prophesied out of an evil spirit, was David's covering.

And it came to pass as they came, when David was returned from the slaughter of the Philistine, that the women came out of all cities of Israel, singing and dancing, to meet king Saul, with tabrets, with joy, and with instruments of music. And the women answered one another as they played, and said, Saul hath slain his thousands, and David his ten thousands. And Saul was very wroth, and the saying displeased him; and he said, They have ascribed unto David ten thousands, and to me they have ascribed but thousands: and what can he have more but the kingdom? And Saul eyed David from that day and forward. And it came to pass on the morrow, that the evil spirit from God came upon Saul, and he prophesied in the midst of the house: and David played with his hand, as at other times: and there was a javelin in Saul's hand. And

Saul cast the javelin; for he said, I will smite David even to the wall with it. And David avoided out of his presence twice. (1 Samuel 18:6–11)

Those who conspire against you are often afraid of the anointing on your life. Saul was afraid of David. "And Saul was afraid of David, because the LORD was with him, and was departed from Saul" (1 Samuel 18:12). In spite of this, the Bible records that "David behaved himself wisely in all his ways; and the LORD was with him" (1 Samuel 18:14). David respected God's anointed king, and despite several opportunities, he refused to harm Saul.

I am by no means implying that you serve under a spiritual covering who wishes to have you killed, although you may feel this way at times. Rather, the story about David and King Saul serves as a reminder that sometimes God calls us to submit to an "evil king." God may be using the evil king to help bring out the good in us by demonstrating the things we should *not* do and attitudes we should *not* have once He promotes us into a leadership role.

King Saul had the honor of being Israel's first king, but his life ended in tragedy for one reason—he did not trust God. Saul became king when he was thirty years old and reigned over Israel for forty-two years. However, early in his career, he made a fatal mistake and disobeyed God by failing to completely destroy the Amalekites and all their possessions as God had commanded. David won numerous battles while serving under King Saul, and King Saul became consumed with jealousy. Instead of building up Israel, jealousy and fear caused King Saul to waste most of his time chasing David through the hills. Because of this, the Lord withdrew his favor from Saul.[2]

While serving under King Saul, David knew the call upon his own life before King Saul even realized it, yet he submitted and went wherever the king sent him. King Saul eventually set David over the men of war, and David became widely accepted in the sight of all the people of Israel. In spite of your current circumstances, know that God is positioning you for favor and greatness. You have already been anointed for the assignment. Your mentor, pastor, or spiritual covering's sole purpose in your life is to launch you into your destiny. The King Saul in your life can't stop your purpose.

Tragically, Saul committed political suicide because he forfeited the kingdom, spiritual suicide because He got out of the will of God, and physical suicide by taking his own life. Only then did David assume his rightful position as king. The King Saul that may be coming against you is, in actuality, digging a hole for his or her own grave.

Do not abort the call of God on your life by depending on your own strength and taking matters into your own hands. God has an assignment that only you can fulfill.

However, God not only needs to know if He can trust you, but He also waits to see if you will trust Him, even if it means serving under an evil king who tries to kill your purpose. Can God trust you not to abort your assignment by cutting off the "skirt" of your leader?

> And the men of David said unto him, Behold the day of which the LORD said unto thee, Behold, I will deliver thine enemy into thine hand, that thou mayest do to him as it shall seem good unto thee. Then David arose, and cut off the skirt of Saul's robe privily. And it came to pass afterward, that David's heart smote him, because he had cut off Saul's skirt. And he said unto his men, The LORD forbid that I should do this thing unto my master, the LORD's anointed, to stretch forth mine hand against him, seeing he is the anointed of the LORD. (1 Samuel 24:4–6)

David's act of cutting away a piece of King Saul's robe is symbolic of the king's mantle being taken away from Saul and given to David before God's *kairos* (perfect) timing. In other words, David took matters into his own hands. The Bible records that afterward "David's heart smote him." He was conscious-stricken because he recognized King Saul as still being God's anointed.

Bishop David C. Cooper once said these words to his leadership staff, which I'll never forget: "You may not respect the person, but you must respect the position." David respected King Saul's position because it was God-assigned. Everyone needs the mantle of their mentor's anointing transferred to them at some point, but in God's timing, not your own.

Send Ananias

When we are new in the prophetic or have not been properly guided in the delivery of a prophetic word, our words may persecute instead of produce. A word that is released too soon and has not fermented in the spirit of a budding prophet or prophetess can instill poison instead of inspire potential.

Even while Saul from Tarsus was persecuting the Christian faith, God saw the potential in him and placed a divine call upon his life to minister with knowledge after conversion and in the same zeal he used before his conversion to Christianity. God sent Ananias to Saul to restore his sight so he could rightly divide the Word of truth.

> The Lord told him [Ananias], "Go to the house of Judas on Straight Street and ask for a man

from Tarsus named Saul, for he is praying. In a vision he has seen a man named Ananias come and place his hands on him to restore his sight." (Acts 9:11–12)

God will send an Ananias into your life to restore prophetic sight, and at the same time, He will also raise you up as an Ananias in the lives of others. We all need an Ananias to show us the truth so we can boldly proclaim the gospel of Jesus Christ accurately. We need an Ananias to remove the scales from our eyes so we can see what the Lord is doing and prophesy with keen insight the Word of the Lord.

Then Ananias went to the house and entered it. Placing his hands on Saul, he said, "Brother Saul, the Lord—Jesus, who appeared to you on the road as you were coming here—has sent me so that you may see again and be filled with the Holy Spirit." Immediately, something like scales fell from Saul's eyes, and he could see again. He got up and was baptized, and after taking some food, he regained his strength. (Acts 9:17–19 NIV)

As prophetic men and women of God, it is important that our zeal does not negate the need for the knowledge of His Word. "Study to shew thyself approved unto God, a workman that needeth not to be ashamed, rightly dividing the word of truth" (2 Timothy 2:15). If we do not know *the* Word, we cannot effectively prophesy *His* Word to anyone else. Our spiritual covering plays an important role in teaching and guiding us and removing the scales from our eyes so we can see the light of God's revelation through His Word. Zeal without knowledge yields no good fruit.

> Brethren, my heart's desire and prayer to God for Israel is, that they might be saved. For I bear them record that they have a zeal of God, but not according to knowledge. For they being ignorant of God's righteousness, and going about to establish their own righteousness, have not submitted themselves unto the righteousness of God. (Romans 10:2–3)

Pastors are called and assigned by God to feed us with manna from heaven so we can mature in the faith and knowledge of our Lord and Savior Jesus Christ and effectively build up His kingdom through the *logos* (written) and *rhema* (revelatory) Word. Father God, send Ananias to touch our eyes so we will see You in all things and speak only what You have ordained for us to utter.

Chapter 6
PROPHETIC TEMPERAMENT

—•—

> What good is it for someone to gain the whole
> world, yet forfeit their soul?
>
> —Mark 8:36 NIV

SELF-MASTERY

Our greatest challenge as a child of God is the mastering of self. It takes thousands of hours to achieve mastery and be considered an expert in a particular field of study. It takes 42,240 hours to be considered an expert in the field of neurosurgery; 13,440 hours in culinary arts; 9,600 hours in sports; and 26,880 hours in astrophysics.[1] Just imagine how many hours it would take to master the self. I would venture to say—a lifetime. Our Father, *Elohim*, is the only one who has the power to use us beyond our own self-mastery. All we need is a desire to be made whole— spirit, soul, and body.

When we accept Jesus as Savior, our unregenerate spirit is reborn, and we become new creations in Him.

God has done a perfect work in us; however, our soul and body are another matter. The soul is the seat of our mind, will, and emotions. Every thought that enters into the mind travels through the soul and affects the body. This is why it is extremely important to guard your thoughts. "Casting down imaginations, and every high thing that exalteth itself against the knowledge of God, and bringing into captivity every thought to the obedience of Christ" (2 Corinthians 10:5).

Allow the Holy Spirit to cover every area of your soul that needs mending; hence, the infilling of the Holy Spirit. The Holy Spirit (God Himself), as teacher and guide, will help us maneuver through this maze called life and successfully destroy the yoke of our fleshly desires. Even the apostle Paul said it this way, "I die daily" (1 Corinthians 15:31). We must lay down our fleshly desires, which enter into the mind through our thoughts, at the altar and allow the Lord to purge us of anything that does not model His character in the earth. The Word of God says, "I beseech you therefore, brethren, by the mercies of God, that ye present your bodies a living sacrifice, holy, acceptable unto God, which is your reasonable service" (Romans 12:1).

Notice in Romans 12:1, the word *bodies* is plural. Therefore, we must present all of our bodies to the Lord—emotional, mental, and physical—as a living sacrifice to Him. Diligence in this area will ensure that as we approach the altar one way, we will not go back the same way. When the wise men presented gifts to Jesus Christ, they were warned by God not to go back the same way they came.

> And when they were come into the house, they saw the young child with Mary his mother, and fell down, and worshipped him: and when they had opened their treasures, they presented unto him gifts; gold, and frankincense and myrrh. And being warned of God in a dream that they should not return to Herod, they departed into their own country another way. (Matthew 2:11–12)

When Saul came among the company of prophets he turned into another man. "And the Spirit of the LORD will come upon thee [Saul], and thou shalt prophesy with them and shalt be turned into another man" (1 Samuel 10:6).

Spending time in the presence of God inevitably changes us. By offering our will, our way, and our works to Him, we cannot remain the same. When we lay our all at the feet of Jesus, God in us will resurrect and become the "ram in the bush" that will fulfill His plan in the earth. Simply because of our submission to His will, way, and works, He will accomplish His plans through us. No longer should you be burdened by pride, fear, anxiety, or the cares of this world because you have laid them down at the altar as your "reasonable service." The Lord is looking for a yielded vessel, not a *shielded* vessel. Once you lay it all down, do not go back to retrieve it.

> "The Lord is looking for a yielded vessel not a shielded vessel.

Prophet Bill Hamon, founder of Christian International, coined the temperament among prophetically gifted people as "Prophetic Mood Swings (PMS)." Dr. Tim Early, founder of Foundations of the Apostles and Prophets International Ministry, has referred to the prophetic temperament as "Programmed Mind-Sets." According to Dr. Early,

PMS is the principle of reaction versus response. Prophets and prophetic people must not let or allow their minds to be clouded by the reaction and opinions of others, or through poor perceptions of what the intended purpose and trial is for in their life. PMS sends up a red flag as to how we, as prophetic people of God, either react or respond to the personal process we are going through and the dealings of God for our progression and maturity.[2]

We must learn to master our own PMS before we even consider ministering to others. If not, we will prophesy out of an erratic emotional body as opposed to a still spirit. "Be still and know that I am God" (Psalm 46:10). Until we can still the mind of background noise and excessive chatter, we cannot fully know the "I AM" aspects of God within us. Whatever follows your prophetic I AM becomes its nature. Therefore, be mindful of your thoughts, as your thoughts will form your words, and your words will define your life.

Be Made Whole

We are the temple of the Holy Spirit. Ministry first begins within us. If we cannot control our mind, will, and emotions, how can we expect to impact nations? The Word of God says, "Physician, heal thyself" (Luke 4:23). We can't heal ourselves if we don't use meditation as our medication. In meditation, we silence the noise within us in order to hear the Lord's whisper. During meditation, we turn the spiritual stethoscope inward, which takes resilience. Letting go of past hurts, inner pain, and secret wounds to reveal open scars that only God can heal takes courage. I am reminded of the woman with the "spirit of infirmity" for eighteen long years:

> And behold, there was a woman which had a spirit of infirmity eighteen years, and was bowed together, and could in no wise lift up herself. And when Jesus saw her, he called her to him and said unto her, Woman, thou art loosed from thine infirmity. And he laid his hands on her: and immediately she was made straight, and glorified God. (Luke 13:11–13)

Imagine seeing the ground of limitation for eighteen years and not being able to stand up straight because of the unrelenting weight and pain of your condition. As prophetic men and women of God, if we have not sought the Lord for healing, we will remain bowed over, only seeing the ground of limitation, and never rising to a higher prophetic realm in Him. The number eighteen can be broken down into the numbers six-six-six, which is the number for the mark of the beast (Revelation 13:18). If we do not seek God for healing, we will prophesy from our beastly (carnal) nature, remaining bowed over in our own infirmities.

We are called to be producers of our future rather than products of our past. We are called to prophesy *from* our past hurts, not *in* them. As ministers, we minister *from* what we have overcome, not *in* who we once were. When we allow the healing of God to make us whole, we can then prophesy *from* that once-broken place rather than *in* it. I am not saying to forget where you have come from, only to allow your past to prophetically push you into a place of wholeness and prophesy from that place.

> And, behold, a woman, which was diseased with an issue of blood twelve years, came behind him, and touched the hem of his garment. For she said within herself, If I may but touch his garment, I shall be whole. But Jesus turned him about, and when he saw her, he said, Daughter, be of good comfort; thy faith hath made thee whole. And the woman was made whole from that hour. (Matthew 9:20–22)

Bishop Clarence McClendon, founder of Clarence E. McClendon Ministries (CEMM) and senior pastor of Full Harvest International Church in Gardena, California, once expounded upon the "hem." He explained that the hem of a garment is the last thing that is done to complete a garment. Once the hem is done, the garment is complete. Therefore, when the woman touched the hem of Jesus' garment, she touched the finished work of Jesus Christ.

I believe God also wants to finish His work in you, but He is waiting for you to activate your faith and touch His hem. Many have accepted the healing anointing of God but have not the finished work. Many return to the altar because they have been *healed* in one area but were not made *whole* in every area of their infirmity. God desires to say to you, "Your faith has made you whole" (Luke 8:48).

After the woman was made whole, she "glorified God." Being made whole will release the spirit of prophecy in you because the "testimony of Jesus is the spirit of prophecy" (Revelation 19:10). The spirit of prophecy is the first level of prophetic operations. Once our faith is activated, and God heals the inner wounds, we can then speak prophetically *from* our wholeness instead of *in* our infirmity. In order to kick-start your faith and be made whole, you must get to a place where your focus is on touching not only His hem but also Him. After touching Him, His healing virtue will then flow through you and enable you to minister healing and wholeness to others through the spirit of prophecy.

Allow the light of God to shine in the dark places of your soul. Don't rehearse a painful past, but release a restored present. As you lay before God, allow Him to perform spiritual heart surgery on you. God is saying, "Be still and know that I am God" (Psalm 46:10). Let go of self, and be confident in knowing that "he who began a good work in you will carry it on to completion until the day of Christ Jesus" (Philippians 1:6 NIV). Listen for His still, small voice to whisper in your ear, "It is finished" (John 19:30). Only then will God release you to release others into their prophetic destiny.

Chapter 7

THE PROPHETIC WORD

In the beginning was the Word, and the Word
was with God, and the Word was God. The same
was in the beginning with God. All things were
made by him; and without him was not anything
made that was made. In him was life; and the life
was the light of men. And the light shineth in
darkness; and the darkness comprehended it not.

—John 1:1–5

The Preexisting Word

The Word embodies all of God. It embodies God the
Father, God the Son, and God the Holy Spirit, as all three-
in-one were with God in the beginning. The moment you
were filled with the Holy Spirit is the moment that God
"breathed into [your] nostrils the breath of life; and [you]
became a living soul" (Genesis 2:7). Therefore, as you
exhale the very breath of God through your prophetic

utterances, the Spirit of God that is attached to the Word is imparting life to the hearers, and they, too, are becoming "living souls."

The Word existed in the beginning and was with God in the beginning; therefore, it is the preexisting, ever-eternal Word. All other words spoken since the beginning are simply an out-birthing of this preexisting Word. The preexisting Word has never changed. The preexisting Word, spoken prophetically, will not stop until it has completed its mission in transforming a fallen humanity into that which was once with God in the beginning. Prophetic in nature, the preexisting Word is continuously in motion, creating new life, renewing minds, and transforming lives.

The preexisting Word is the person of Jesus Christ, who was with God in the beginning and was "made flesh, and dwelt among us (and we beheld his glory, the glory as of the only begotten of the Father,) full of grace and truth" (John 1:14). If we are prophesying outside of the nature of the preexisting Word, Jesus Christ, we are speaking from a door of divination instead of through the door of Jesus. The Hebrew word for *divination* is *qecem,* meaning a lot; oracle: reward of divination, divine sentence, witchcraft. It is from the root word *qacam*, which means to distribute; determine by lot or magical scroll; diviner, prudent, soothsayer, use divination.[1] Gaining hidden knowledge and insight from other gods is divination. Using techniques other than praying to our Father in heaven to learn secret information or the future is divination. The Word of God clearly warns against its use.

> When you enter the land which the LORD your God gives you, you shall not learn to imitate the detestable things of those nations. There shall not be found among you anyone who makes his son or his daughter pass through the fire, one who uses divination, one who practices witchcraft, or one who interprets omens, or a sorcerer, or one who casts a spell, or a medium or a spiritist, or one who calls up the dead. (Deuteronomy 18:9–11 NASB)

Practicing divination places one in the realm of deceptive spirits, causing many to "fall away from the faith." The apostle Paul predicted, "But the Spirit explicitly says that in later times some will fall away from the faith, paying attention to deceitful spirits and doctrines of demons" (1Timothy 4:1 NASB). We are in the last days, and the devil is seeking to deceive all who will yield to his lies. To deceive is to make someone believe something that is not true. We must guard against deception by keeping our prophetic antennae fully extended to discern the truth from the lie (the deception). The Word of God says, "For there shall arise false Christs, and false prophets, and shall shew great signs and wonders; insomuch that, if possible, they shall deceive the very elect" (Matthew 24:24). Notice the Scripture says, "if possible." As long as we remain rooted and ground in His Word, it is *not* possible because His Word will keep us in the truth and away from the bondage resulting from deception.

Jesus said, "I am the door: by me if any man enters in, he shall be saved, and shall go in and out and find pasture" (John 10:9). Prophesying through any other door outside of *the* door, Jesus Christ, is divination and comes from a psychic realm, as opposed to the prophetic realm from which the preexisting Word is outbirthed. Prophesying outside of the door leaves one in a place of want: always thirsty, always unfulfilled, and never truly satisfied. Those prophesying outside of *the* door, Jesus Christ, cannot "go in and out and find pasture" because they are trapped inside a locked door. It is imperative that we maintain access to the kingdom of heaven through the door of Jesus Christ. Christ has given every believer the keys. "And I will give unto thee the keys of the kingdom of heaven: and whatsoever thou shalt bind on earth shall be bound in heaven: and whatsoever thou shalt loose on earth shall be loosed in heaven" (Matthew 16:19).

Our prophetic word should point people to: 1) Jesus Christ—the Way; 2) Jesus Christ— the Truth; and 3)

Jesus Christ—the Life. "I am the way and the truth and the life. No one comes to the Father except through me. If you really knew me, you would know my Father as well. From now on, you do know him and have seen him" (John 14:6–7 NIV).

If anyone speaks a word into your life that steers you away from Jesus Christ or a word that is not in agreement with *the* Word, it is a false word, having no life in itself. Jesus Christ, the preexisting Word, transcended from heaven, wrapped in flesh, to become the ultimate sacrificial lamb for our sins as spoken prophetically by the prophets of old. Jesus Christ is the fulfillment of Old Testament prophecy.

But he was wounded for our transgressions, he was bruised for our iniquities: the chastisement of our peace was upon him; and with his stripes we are healed. All we like sheep have gone astray; we have turned everyone to his own way; and the LORD hath laid on him the iniquity of us all. He was oppressed, and he was afflicted, yet he opened not his mouth: he is brought as a lamb to the slaughter, and as a sheep before her shearers is dumb, so he openeth not his mouth. He was taken from prison and from judgment: and who shall declare his generation? for he was cut off out of the land of the living: for the transgression of my people was he stricken. And he made his grave with the wicked, and with the rich in his death; because he had done no violence, neither was any deceit in his mouth. Yet it pleased the LORD to bruise him; he hath put him to grief: when thou shalt make his soul an offering for sin, he shall see his seed, he shall prolong his days, and the pleasure of the LORD shall prosper in his hand. He shall see of the travail of his soul, and shall be satisfied: by his knowledge shall my righteous servant justify many; for he shall bear their iniquities. Therefore will I divide him a portion with the great, and he shall divide the spoil with the strong; because he hath poured out his soul unto death: and he was numbered with the transgressors; and he bare the sin of many, and made intercession for the transgressors. (Isaiah 53:5–12)

Jesus Christ, the preexisting Word who was with God in the beginning, became the Word for many of us in the earth realm by which everyone must believe in order to receive everlasting life. "For God so loved the world, that he gave his only begotten Son, that whosoever believeth in him should not perish, but have everlasting life" (John 3:16).

The Word that comes from God Himself will leave heaven, come to earth, and work for you. In like manner, the prophetic word spoken through you into the lives of others will leave heaven, come to earth, and work for them.

GOD'S WORD IS TRUTH

> "Sanctify them through thy truth: thy word is truth. As thou hast sent me into the world, even so have I also sent them into the world. And for their sakes I sanctify myself, that they also might be sanctified through the truth" (John 17:17–19).

We are sanctified, or set apart, through the truth of God's Word that resides in us. Truth is an active ingredient that causes the Word of God to perform in the life of a believer because the truth of His Word cannot lie. God's Word cannot return back to Him void because it is submerged in truth. His Word will remain active throughout generations until it has accomplished that which it was sent to accomplish. "So shall my word be that goeth forth out of my mouth: it shall not return unto me void, but it shall accomplish that which I please, and it shall prosper in the thing whereto I sent it" (Isaiah 55:11).

In order for His word to "accomplish," it must first be sent; and God uses fallible people to send His infallible

Word. The Word of God declares, "He sent His word, and healed them, and delivered them from their destructions" (Psalm 107:20). Anyone who speaks a presumptuous word that God has not sent is at that moment being used as an agent of the devil and not an advocate for truth.

> Then the LORD said to me, "These prophets are telling lies in my name. I did not send them or tell them to speak. I did not give them any messages. They prophesy of visions and revelations they have never seen or heard. They speak foolishness made up in their own lying hearts." (Jeremiah 14:14 NLT)

There is no truth that can be found within a lie because a lie comes from the father of lies.

> Ye are of your father the devil, and the lusts of your father ye will do. He was a murderer from the beginning, and abode not in the truth, because there is no truth in him. When he speaketh a lie, he speaketh of his own: for he is a liar, and the father of it. (John 8:44)

Just as there is no truth found within a lie, no light can be found in darkness. In fact, light has a twofold purpose—it exposes and it guides. It exposes that which is hidden in the dark and can also guide one out of the darkness. Many who are prophetic will find the light of God in them exposing the evil prowling around in the darkness simply through their mere presence. They also understand that the same light in them can guide others into their preordained prophetic promises.

When I was a child, the church mothers led a congregational hymn entitled, "This Little Light of Mine." Everyone would join the mothers, all singing in unison and with such a joyful spirit. However, as I grew older and began to study the Word for myself, I soon realized that our light is not little. In fact, it is huge and cannot be hidden.

> You are the light of the world. A city set on a hill cannot be hidden. Nor do people light a lamp and put it under a basket, but on a stand, and it gives light to all in the house. In the same way, let your light shine before others, so that they may see your good works and give glory to your Father who is in heaven. (Matthew 5:14–16 ESV)

Let the light of God in you shine. God is sending prophetic men and women to shine the light of His truth into the dark crevices of the earth.

Now Faith

Because God's Word is active throughout generations, inherent within it must be the element of faith. The Word of God says, "Now faith is the substance of things hoped for, the evidence of things not seen" (Hebrews 11:1). As prophetical people, we typically see or hear the Word as it is unfolding. We see or hear it in that "now" moment in time, regardless of whether it is a prophetic word about the past, present, or future, because the prophetic word does not discern time. It is endowed with "now" faith that is timeless and immeasurable. "Now" faith is also substantive, meaning, there is already evidence of it in the heavens. "Now" faith, spoken prophetically, initiates the process of bringing this evidence from the heavenly realm into the earthly realm to be seen openly. "Now" faith gives thrust to the prophetic word and drives it into action and demonstration.

"Worlds were framed" using the element of "now" faith. "Through faith we understand that the worlds were framed by the word of God, so that things which are seen were not made of things which do appear" (Hebrews 11:3). We must recognize and know that resident within us is enough faith to "frame a world," for God has given each of us "the measure of faith" (Romans 12:3). Even the life in which we now live in the flesh we live by the faith of the Son of God who loved us and gave Himself for us (Galatians 2:20).

Years ago, the Lord gave me this simple definition of faith. He said, "Faith is the supernatural ability to see in the dark." There will come a point in your prophetic walk where God will enable you to "see" from deep within the dark depths of your "pot of transformation." At this point, you have learned to rely on His "now" faith and can use it prophetically to decree and declare His Word to others.

> "Faith is the supernatural ability to see in the dark.

Although our faith cannot be depleted to nothingness, it can become weakened. During those times when our faith is weak, we must learn to totally trust God and rely on the measure of faith that is innate within His Word, which will strengthen us as well as those to whom we are assigned to minister. Even the apostles had those moments when their faith had grown weak: "The apostles said unto the Lord, increase our faith!" (Luke 17:5) Only God, through His Word, can increase the strength of our faith.

THE WORD OF HIS POWER

Power is an inherent characteristic of God the Father, God the Son, and God the Holy Spirit. It is the result of God's nature, which can be seen in His creation.

> Long ago, at many times and in many ways, God spoke to our fathers by the prophets, but in these last days he has spoken to us by his Son, whom he appointed the heir of all things, through whom also he created the world. He is the radiance of the glory of God and the exact imprint of his nature, and he upholds the universe by the word of his power. (Hebrews 1:1–3a ESV)

When Jesus Christ, who is the "exact imprint of His [God's] nature," came to earth as the only begotten Son of the Father, He displayed both intrinsic (inherent) and derived aspects of power. The intrinsic power of Jesus Christ is demonstrated in the fact that He is God in the flesh. He is the embodiment of the divine nature of God. "I and my Father are one" (John 10:30). The power of Jesus Christ is demonstrated because it is derived, or passed down, from the Father. "And Jesus came and spake unto them, saying, All power is given unto me in heaven and in earth" (Matthew 28:18).

In the single person of Jesus, He has both a divine and a human nature. He is all God and all man. His divine nature was not changed when the Word became flesh. Instead, the Word was joined with humanity.[2] Since we are "partakers of His divine nature" (2 Peter 1:4), the power and authority to use His name has been passed down to us as Spirit-filled believers of Jesus Christ. The Word of God tells us that "at the name of Jesus every knee should bow, of things in heaven, and things in earth, and things under the earth" (Philippians 2:10). There is power in the name of Jesus, and we have been deputized, as Spirit-filled, born-again believers, to use His name. In His name, we can cast out demons; lay hands on the sick and they will recover; set at liberty those who are bound; create an atmosphere for miracles, signs, and wonders; and speak to the mountains (obstacles) and command them to move. Yes, there is wonder-working power in the name of Jesus, and God distributes His power (derived) to every believer. "Behold, I give unto you power to tread on serpents and scorpions, and over all the power of the enemy: and nothing shall by any means hurt you" (Luke 10:19).

The dynamic of God's power is conveyed throughout the Word. His power is far from passive in nature and remains active through us. The power that is innate within God's Word produces evidence of productivity. Stay connected to *the* power source—God.

The prophetic word of God is relevant today. It has not stopped creating and is the manna from heaven that sustains us. The Word carries with it truth that will silence lies, light that will dispel darkness, faith to produce evidence, and power to work miracles. Therefore, as prophetic men and women of God, we have a responsibility to minister the prophetic word of the Lord to whomever He sends.

Chapter 8

PROPHETIC ELEVATION

———•◦•———

I know thy works: behold, I have set before thee an open door, and no man can shut it: for thou hast a little strength, and has kept my word, and has not denied my name.

—Revelation 3:8

Doors Are Opening

Doors are opening for you that no man can shut, because you have obeyed God and have not denied His name. Each door carries with it increased responsibility, but God will grace you with supernatural strength to walk through. As you are elevated, more and more of your self-will dies to the point where you are totally reliant upon God's strength and not your own.

God may even give you a glimpse of what is waiting for you behind each door. This glimpse may come through a prophetic word; through reading His Word; or through people, angels, dreams, or open visions. He may not be taking you to the pulpit or onto a national platform. Behind one door, God may be calling you to minister to that one person on the street corner who has lost all hope. Behind another door, a family living in a homeless shelter may need an answer or direction for their lives. Behind the next door, someone bound by drugs may need you to minister a word of deliverance. Behind another approaching door, the pastor of a small church in the backwoods of Mississippi may need you to serve as a midwife to help him or her give birth to God's vision for the house.

Yes, the doors of the church are open because God is calling you beyond the usual four walls of church to minister to those who may not look like you, act like you, smell like you, or even talk like you. Yes, the door leading to your prophetic elevation carries with it a weight for which only a shift into a new anointing can strengthen you.

ELEVATED TO SERVE

"His lord said unto him, Well done, good and faithful servant; thou hast been faithful over a few things, I will make thee ruler over many things: enter thou into the joy of thy lord" (Matthew 25:23).

The highest form of elevation is experienced through serving. Elisha was elevated in the prophetic as a result of his service to Elijah, and he received a double portion of Elijah's anointing. Who are you serving? The "double portion" comes from those the Lord has assigned for you to serve, and you will need it to sustain you as you walk through the open doors God will place before you.

Jesus' mission as He walked the earth was a life of service to others, and even after His death, burial, and resurrection, He is still serving. "For even the Son of Man did not come to be served, but to serve, and to give his life as a ransom for many" (Mark 10:45 NIV). Jesus washed His disciples' feet as an act of service and as an example for everyone to follow.

> So after he had washed their feet, and had taken his garments, and was set down again, he said unto them, Know ye what I have done to you? Ye call me Master and Lord: and ye say well; for so I am. If I then, your Lord and Master, have washed your feet; ye also ought to wash one another's feet. For I have given you an example, that ye should do as I have done to you. Verily, verily, I say unto you, The servant is not greater than his lord; neither he that is sent greater than he that sent him. If ye know these things, happy are ye if ye do them. (John 13:12–17)

True servants understand their role in the kingdom. They understand that in order to become a great leader, one must first be an even greater servant. They understand the value of serving others behind the scenes. Although their seed of service is planted in secret, God will reward them openly. We must understand that no one is greater than or less than anyone else because of title, position, years in the church or of salvation, spiritual gifts, or a divine call. We are all called to be servants (ministers) one to another: "Submitting yourselves one to another in the fear of God" (Ephesians 5:21). There is no ranking system in the kingdom of God. In fact, the Word of God says, "In the same way, the last will be first, and the first will be last, because many are called, but few are chosen" (Matthew 20:16 ISV).

We as Christian believers have a common purpose: to occupy until He comes. Remain poised to serve regardless of title or position and resolve to "do nothing from selfish ambition or conceit, but in humility count others more significant than yourselves" (Philippians 2:3 NIV).

Heart of Humility

When I was a child growing up, the deacons of the church I attended would usually begin their opening prayer with "Father, we come to you as humbly as we know how."

Humility is the key to elevation and promotion. Humility is defined as "the quality or state of not thinking you are better than other people, the quality or state of being humble or not proud."[1] Jesus Christ "humbled himself, and became obedient unto death, even the death of the cross" (Philippians 2:8). We, too, must humble ourselves and obey God.

Humility comes from the heart and is demonstrated by consistent obedience. Humility is not a weak emotion but rather is the outward showing of one's inner strength. As prophetic people, the Lord teaches us lessons in humility throughout our prophetic walk, and these lessons most often come in the form of life experiences. The negative experiences we walk through in life are designed to make us by increasing and strengthening our inner man. The Word of God tells us that "He [Christ] learned obedience by the things which he suffered" (Hebrews 5:8).

Obedience comes through suffering and is demonstrated in humility. But "after you have suffered awhile, the God of all grace will himself restore, confirm, strengthen, and establish you" (1 Peter 5:10 ESV). This is prophetic elevation.

Everything that happens to us has been given permission, by God, to happen. The Master Teacher knows exactly when His students are ready for each test along their prophetic walk. Remember His servant Job? "And the Lord said unto Satan, Hast thou considered my servant Job, that there is none like him in the earth, a perfect and an upright man, one that feareth God and escheweth evil?" (Job 1:8)

God teaches us how to see each test from His perspective. One of the signals that we are being elevated from one dimension in the Spirit to another or from glory to glory and faith to faith is when our perspective becomes aligned with His perspective while we are going through the tests. Your vantage point, spiritually, will determine how each test is perceived and handled. "[God] will not suffer you to be tempted above that ye are able; but will with the temptation also make a way to escape, that ye may be able to bear it" (1 Corinthians 10:13). Are you focusing on the test when, in fact, your vantage point is such that you can see the escape route? As my mom would say, "Don't add fuel to the fire (test) [by focusing on and constantly discussing the fire] because it only makes the fire bigger." Focus on the escape. The escape is the open door leading to your next elevation.

We must also be very careful not to become pompous prophetics as God raises us up as His mouthpiece in the earth. The Lord detests a proud heart. "Everyone that is proud in heart is an abomination to the LORD: though hand join in hand, he shall not be unpunished" (Proverbs 16:5). A proud heart can delay prophetic elevation.

A person who does not have a servant's heart will not experience the full benefits of

> "*A proud heart can delay prophetic elevation.*

God's blessings. When you serve God by serving others, the Lord will begin to serve you. Never lose focus and think you are serving the man or woman of God. You are actually serving God Himself. Man will disappoint you, but God never will. Don't expect accolades from man; expect acknowledgments from God. Don't expect man to recognize your service; expect God to reward you for your service. The Word of God says, "And let us not be weary in well doing: for in due season we shall reap, if we faint not" (Galatians 6:9).

THE FOUNDATION

Now therefore ye are no more strangers and foreigners, but fellow citizens with the saints, and of the household of God; And are built upon the foundation of the apostle and prophets, Jesus Christ himself being the chief corner stone; In whom all the building fitly framed together groweth unto an holy temple in the Lord. In whom

ye also are builded together for an habitation of
God through the Spirit. (Ephesians 2:19–22)

Elevation starts from a foundation. The apostles and
prophets are the foundation from which all the essential
elements of the church are built, and Jesus Christ is the
"bonding glue" that holds these elements together. The
foundation is the first part of the structure to be poured and
leveled after the ground has been broken. The foundation
undergoes the greatest inconveniences throughout the
building process because it is constantly being stepped on
and seemingly disregarded. There is also a period of time
in which the foundation is exposed to the outside elements
of nature, such as rain, sleet, snow, and ice. Nevertheless,
the foundation is the strongest part of the structure, built
to withstand the elements and designed to carry the load
of all the materials used to complete the building.

For those who are called into the apostolic or prophetic
offices, God has anointed you to withstand the elements
that life throws your way and to bear the load of others.
We are connected to the building (those we serve). As the
building rises, we rise. As the building is elevated, we are
also elevated because of our connection to the building.
Every element of the building is needed.

ASCEND

At each step along our prophetic walk, the Lord is calling us to come up higher in Him. Elevation in the prophetic is accompanied with spiritual ascension. After the crucifixion and burial of Jesus Christ, He *ascended* into heaven. "Who is he that condemneth? It is Christ that died, yea rather, that is risen again, who is even at the right hand of God, who also maketh intercession for us" (Romans 8:34).

Even as Christ ascended to the Father and is at God's right hand, always making intercession for us, we must also ascend. We must ascend spiritually, connect to our Father in heaven, and make intercession for His people— saved and unsaved. We must ascend to a place where prophetic prayers (intercession) come from our spirit and travel into the deep parts of the earth to root out anything that is not like God. Prophetic prayers are downloaded into our spirit from the throne room of heaven. To receive them, we first must yield ourselves to ascend into His presence and enter into that place of prophetic worship, beyond the veil.

Prophetic prayers can cover a wide array of areas. It depends upon the specific burden the Lord has placed in your spirit. Some may be led to pray prophetically for territories, regions, governmental leaders, and school grounds. Others may be led to pray for nations. Others may have a burden and sudden travail for those who are sick, lame, and destitute. Some may be prompted to pray for those who serve in ministry. As we ascend, we become as prophetic watchmen on the walls. "O Jerusalem, I have posted watchmen on your walls; they will pray day and night, continually. Take no rest, all you who pray to the LORD" (Isaiah 62:6 NLT). Prophetic prayers of the watchmen are not rehearsed; they are birthed. The birthing comes from a place where we have ascended, through the guidance of the Holy Spirit, to hear the Lord's whisper.

KEEP SERVING

When I was a child, every so often my mom would sing "Serving the Lord," written by William Morganfield, Sammy Stevens, and Kenneth Morris:

> Serving the Lord will pay off afterwhile.
> Serving God I know it will pay off afterwhile.
> Just keep working everyday;
> Whatever is right, God said He'll pay.
> Serving the Lord, I know it's going
> to pay off after while. [2]

This song was later coined by a few in the congregation as my mom's signature song. Back then, I was just a listener, but now I am living those lyrics that will forever resonate in my spirit.

Keep serving, for you will reap a harvest in due season. Keep serving, for God will cause increase to meet you at your doorstep. Your labor is not in vain. "Therefore, my beloved brethren, be steadfast, unmovable, always abounding in the work of the Lord, forasmuch as ye know that your labour is not in vain in the Lord" (1 Corinthians 15:58).

While you are serving, stay prayerful. Ask the Lord to lead you as you serve. God will not steer you in the wrong direction. Never allow the "accuser of the brethren" to whisper insecurities in your ear about the one you are serving. Serve with all diligence, honor, and humility. Be the gift of prophecy (edification, exhortation, and comfort) to the one you are serving, and experience prophetic elevation as a result of your faithfulness.

CHAPTER 9

THE PROPHETIC REALM

And it shall come to pass in the last days, saith God, I will pour out of my Spirit upon all flesh: and your sons and your daughters shall prophesy, and your young men shall see visions, and your old men shall dream dreams.

—Acts 2:17

THE HOLY SPIRIT

The baptism of the Holy Spirit is the doorway into the prophetic realm. The Holy Spirit is an all-knowing and all-seeing Spirit who shares with Spirit-filled believers past, present, and future events regarding people, places, and/or things. This same Spirit also gives to the believer the power to change the atmosphere and to create our present and our future conditions simply by speaking His Word. The Holy Spirit is a prophetic Spirit.

And when the day of Pentecost was fully come, they were all with one accord in one place. And suddenly there came a sound from heaven as of a rushing mighty wind, and it filled all the house where they were sitting. And there appeared unto them cloven tongues like as of fire, and it sat upon each of them. And they were all filled with the Holy Ghost, and began to speak with other tongues, as the Spirit gave them utterance ... And they were all amazed and marveled, saying one to another, Behold are not all these which speak Galileans? And how hear we every man in our own tongue, wherein we were born? (Acts 2:1–4, 7–8)

> "The baptism of the Holy Spirit is the doorway into the prophetic realm.

In Acts 2, the Holy Spirit "sat upon each of them, and they were filled with the Holy Ghost and began to speak with other tongues, as the Spirit gave them utterance." As you move in the prophetic realm, the Spirit of God will give you the utterance for His people if you are at one with Him in mind, body, soul, and spirit. The Word of

God asks, "Can two walk together without agreeing on the direction?" (Amos 3:3 NLT) The answer is no. When you are in one accord with God, you will speak from one distinct heavenly sound—one chord.

INSPIRED UTTERANCE

> For if I pray in an unknown tongue, my spirit prayeth, but my understanding is unfruitful. What is it then: I will pray with the spirit, and I will pray with the understanding also: I will sing with the spirit, and I will sing with the understanding also. (1 Corinthians 14:14–15)

God-inspired utterances in a known tongue is prophecy. There are various illustrations of prophecy (inspired utterance) that can be demonstrated through a believer, such as teaching, preaching, and evangelizing.

Teaching is prophecy. As the Word is being taught, the Lord downloads into the spirit of the teacher revelation pertaining to the Scriptures. This revelation is then delivered by the teacher under the inspiration of the Holy Spirit, which is inspired utterance in a known tongue (prophecy). Preaching is prophecy because preaching is a proclamation of the gospel under the inspiration of the Holy Spirit. Evangelizing is prophecy because it is witnessing to the nonbeliever the good news of Jesus Christ under the guidance of the Holy Spirit.

Inspired utterances are anointed by God. Inspired utterances can destroy idols, tear down walls of religion, and cause praises to erupt that will literally drive out demons. "The heathen raged, the kingdoms were moved: he uttered his voice, the earth melted" (Psalm 46:6). In other words, the earth responds when God's voice speaks through inspired utterances from the believer. All believers are prophetical because all believers have inspiration residing in them in the person of the Holy Spirit.

PURPOSE AND DELIVERY

Graham Cooke identifies in his book *Approaching the Heart of Prophecy* a number of purposes for prophecy. A few of them are: 1) Prophecy can bring correction and warning, 2) Prophecy opens the teaching of the Word and confirms preaching, and 3) Prophecy can provide direction and enhance vision.[1]

In addition to those few purposes, the Word of God states that prophecy is for edification, exhortation, and comfort: "But he that prophesieth speaketh unto men to edification, and exhortation, and comfort" (1 Corinthians 14:3). Edification means to build up, exhortation means to encourage, and comfort means to console. Prophecy ultimately builds up, encourages, and consoles believers and nonbelievers alike. Prophecy has the potential to move one from being a hearer of the Word to becoming a doer of the Word. It can also motivate the hearers to finish the race before them. Prophecy comes from the heavens and can cause a breakthrough in one's life.

Prophecy, divinely inspired utterance, can occur in two ways. The Holy Spirit can "drop" the Word in your spirit or the Word can "bubble up" from your spirit. The word *drop* in Hebrew is *nataph*, meaning to ooze, to distill gradually, to fall in drops, or to speak by inspiration. The Word declares that the heavens *dropped* at the presence of God.[2] "The earth shook, the heavens also dropped at the presence of God: even Sinai itself was moved at the presence of God, the God of Israel" (Psalm 68:8).

The Word of God also tells us that the heavens declare the glory of God. "The heavens declare the glory of God; the skies proclaim the work of His hands" (Psalm 19:1 NIV). As a prophetical people, we must always be positioned to receive what the heavens are saying, because the heavens are making declarations about God's glory (Psalm 19:1). As God's prophetic mouthpiece in the earth, we must be in a posture to receive His glory as it fills the temple. As the heavens "drop," we should become so wrapped in His glory and caught up in an angelic realm that if we listened closely, we could hear the angels singing. Your prophetic utterance will come as you enter into His presence and speak the Word of the Lord as it is "dropped" into your spirit.

Inspired utterance can also "bubble up" from within your spirit. "Bubble up" in Hebrew is *naba,* which means to speak or sing by inspiration. The Word carries the sense of bubbling or springing up, flowing, pouring out, or gushing forth.[3] "He that believeth on me, as the scripture hath said, out of his belly shall flow rivers of living water" (John 7:38). As you yield to God, out of your "belly" will flow "rivers of living water"— inspired utterance. There is no dry season in your belly because God's rivers are eternal, everlasting, always flowing, and bringing life to those who are willing to drink of the water that He provides. Those who drink of the living water will never thirst again. "But whosoever drinketh of the water that I shall give him shall never thirst; but the water that I shall give him shall be in him a well of water springing up into everlasting life" (John 4:14).

In the natural, water aids in removing toxins from the system. It helps fight infection, reduces cancer risks, and promotes a healthy heart. These are only a few of the benefits of drinking water. Just imagine the benefits of the living water God has placed on the inside of you to give to those who thirst. In you is the living water that can heal a nation. In you is the key to everlasting life, waiting to be poured out and released into the lives of His people. As inspired utterances bubble up within your spirit man, release it in accordance with the prophetic protocol that has been established by the pastor of the local church body.

God-inspired utterance in a known tongue (prophecy) edifies, exhorts, comforts, and brings new life to those who feel as though they have been defeated by life. Inspired utterance can be spoken out of the mouth of every Spirit-filled believer who has yielded him- or herself to God. Prophecy is crucial in the advancement of God's kingdom agenda in the earth. It is too important to be disregarded and not actively operating within

> "*In you is the living water that can heal a nation.*

today's church. Prophecy is also necessary for the unchurched, those who do not frequent the four walls of a church building and are in need of salvation. "Quench not the Spirit. Despise not prophesying" (1 Thessalonians 5:19–20). The living water God has placed in the spirit of a prophetic man or woman of God must not be quenched, and prophecy must not be despised because it has the power to save lives.

LEVELS OF PROPHECY

There are three levels of prophecy: 1) The spirit of prophecy, 2) the gift of prophecy, and 3) the office of the prophet. Each of these levels will be expounded upon in the following sections.

The Spirit of Prophecy

> "Then I fell down at his feet to worship him, but he said to me, 'You must not do that! I am a fellow servant with you and your brothers who hold to the testimony of Jesus. Worship God.' For the testimony of Jesus is the spirit of prophecy" (Revelation 19:10 NASB).

The spirit of prophecy is the testimony of Jesus Christ. Since the spirit of prophecy is the testimony of Jesus, the Word itself carries within itself the spirit of prophecy. The entire Word of God is a testament of Jesus Christ through whom everyone who believes in Him will receive salvation.

All believers can speak under the spirit of prophecy because they are carriers of His Word. When the believer testifies about the goodness of Jesus, he or she is speaking under the spirit of prophecy. When you communicate about His goodness to a coworker, stranger, or neighbor, you are speaking under the spirit of prophecy. When you encourage someone with the Word of God, you are speaking under the spirit of prophecy. You are prophetical in nature because you have the Spirit of God in you, and that same Spirit will quicken you to prophesy under the spirit of prophecy. "But if the Spirit of him that raised up Jesus from the dead dwell in you, he that raised up Christ from the dead shall also quicken your mortal bodies by his Spirit that dwelleth in you" (Romans 8:11).

The Gift of Prophecy

The second level of prophecy is the gift of prophecy. This gift is spoken through Spirit-filled believers to bring edification, exhortation, and comfort to the body of Christ, as mentioned earlier. However, this particular gift carries with it a greater measure of grace and authority, which will be discussed later. Paul admonishes the believer to "Follow after charity, and desire spiritual gifts, but rather that ye may prophesy" (1 Corinthians 14:1). There is nothing wrong with desiring spiritual gifts and to prophesy, but always remember that God is the giver of the gifts, not man.

> Ask, and it shall be given you; seek, and ye shall find; knock, and it shall be opened unto you ...

If ye then, being evil, know how to give good gifts unto your children, how much more shall your Father which is in heaven give good things to them that ask him? (Matthew 7:7, 11)

Never seek or expect a man or woman of God, who may be anointed, blessed, highly favored, and well seasoned in their gift or office, to give to you what only God can. Seek God for revelation and understanding with regard to all of the spiritual gifts. As you are seeking Him, He will send those who are ordained to be in your life to help you discover the gifts He has placed within you. God used the apostle Paul to confirm the gift He had placed within his spiritual son Timothy and to release him into the ministry.

I remember our genuine faith, for you share the faith that first filled your grandmother Lois and your mother, Eunice. And I know that same faith continues strong in you. This is why I remind you to fan into flames the spiritual gift God gave you when I laid my hands on you. (2 Timothy 1:5–6 NLT)

Your spiritual covering serves as a conduit for the activation of the spiritual gifts that were imparted to you by God. Your spiritual covering will encourage you by reminding you to "fan into flames" those gifts. It is important to know what your spiritual gifts are and to begin to utilize them in the body of Christ. A detailed listing and description of the spiritual gifts has been included in the Appendix.

The gift of prophecy must only be delivered within the boundary of grace that has been defined by the Lord. Apostle Eckhardt defines grace as "God's ability, which is our boundary."[4] The gift of prophecy carries with it a greater measure of authority and will have the strongest utterances than one who speaks by the spirit of prophecy. As the believer begins to "fan into flames" the prophetic gift, the utterance becomes stronger because the believer is speaking from the gift. Any believer who attempts to go beyond their level of grace without additional equipping may bring confusion to the body. "God is not the author of confusion, but of peace, as in all churches of the saints" (1 Corinthians 14:33).

Let me take a moment to share a practical example of the importance of operating in your gifts within God's boundary of grace, using my personal experience as a private pilot. In unpressurized aircraft, supplemental oxygen has to be used if pilots fly more than thirty minutes at cabin pressure altitudes of 12,500 feet or higher. At cabin altitudes above fourteen thousand feet, pilots must use oxygen at all times. Above fifteen thousand feet, each occupant of the aircraft must be provided supplemental oxygen. If I am flying above 12,500 feet and portable oxygen is not located on my airplane, I have created an unsafe flying condition. I, and anyone flying with me, could die from oxygen deficiency, or hypoxia, because we are flying beyond the aircraft's safety boundary or grace limits. Even though I am a certified pilot, I have a responsibility to know and comply with the safety limitations for my type aircraft as outlined in the Pilot's Operating Handbook.

In like fashion, although the gift of prophecy may flow through you, you also have a responsibility to be aware of your limitations, or grace-boundary, as outlined in your operating handbook, the Holy Bible. Those who operate in the gift of prophecy "speaketh unto men to edification, and exhortation, and comfort" (1 Corinthians 14:3), and they stay within those three realms.

The Office of the Prophet

The third level of prophecy is the office of the prophet, the highest level in the prophetic realm.

Those who are called into the office of the prophet have been given the supernatural ability to usher God's people into a greater degree of His glory. At this level, the prophet or prophetess ministers to a wider and broader scope of individual needs. Those called into the office of the prophet have the strongest prophetic utterances because they speak by the spirit of prophecy, the gift of prophecy, and also out of the strength of the office. Unlike those with the gift of prophecy, prophecies spoken from a prophet or prophetess extend beyond edification, exhortation, and comfort and further carries with it revelation, direction, correction, confirmation, impartation, and activation.[5]

When God called and ordained the prophet Jeremiah, he said these words: "See, I have this day set thee over the nations and over the kingdoms, to root out, and to pull down, and to destroy, and to throw down, to build, and to plant" (Jeremiah 1:10). Those who are called into this sacred office must realize the power of their words. In their prophetic utterances, although the word may be a hard saying, it should always end with building up and planting. The prophet is called to root out and then plant. The prophet is called to pull down and then pull up. The prophet is called to destroy and then restore. The prophet is called to throw down and then build up.

Again, a prophetic word spoken from the mouth of the prophet or prophetess should end with the building up of the body. We are called to help develop and not damage the body of Christ. We are called to instill faith into the body of Christ, not fear. We are called to show the way to prosperity, not lack. We are called to point them to Jesus Christ, not the enemy.

We have a great responsibility to the body of Christ as prophets and prophetesses. As God's mouthpiece in the earth, we must speak the mind of Christ with the heart of God.

One Body

> And He gave some, apostles; and some, prophets; and some, evangelists; and some, pastors and teachers; for the perfecting of the saints, for the work of the ministry, for the edifying of the body of Christ: Till we all come in the unity of the faith, and of the knowledge of the Son of God, unto a perfect man, unto the measure of the stature of the fullness of Christ. (Ephesians 4:11–13)

The new leadership model for the church can be found in the above passage. These leadership positions are commonly referred to as the "Fivefold Ministry Offices," but this is an incorrect reference because the pastor and teacher are mentioned in Scripture as a single unit. The Greek word *kai* is used to combine them and treat them as one, so in actuality this is a fourfold leadership model.

In addition, the positions are also not simply titles but ministry functions or job descriptions. Their primary responsibility is to prepare God's people for works of service and to build up the body of Christ. Every ministry is an out-branching of the ministry of Christ Himself, who is the chief cornerstone of their foundation. Christ is our chief apostle (Hebrews 3:1), our chief prophet (Luke 24:19), our chief evangelist (Matthew 9:35), our chief pastor (1 Peter 5:2–4), and our chief teacher (John 3:2). Keep in mind, the fivefold ministry leadership model is temporary. Christ's leadership is, and will always be, eternal.[6]

As one commentator explains, the human hand is a simple analogy that illustrates the fivefold ministry office. All of the fingers are of equal importance.

The thumb, which reaches all the other fingers, represents the apostolic ministry. It is the one of government and in working together with others in their unique talents and gifting with wisdom, love, and understanding. The thumb is analogous with the word *govern.* Next to the apostle thumb is the forefinger, which is the prophet finger. It works together with the apostle in the foundational structure or ministries (Ephesians 2:20). Both the ministry of the apostle and prophet are foundational in their emphasis, and because of this, all other materials and structures associated with the building 'rests' upon them. The ministry of the prophet draws the body of Christ closer to Himself and calls the church unto purity and truth. Therefore, the forefinger is one of being a *guide* to others. The middle finger, the longest of all the fingers, has been called the finger of the evangelist. It is far reaching which identifies with the evangelist's ability to gather in the people and spread the gospel. The word *gather* is used for this finger. Next to the middle finger is the ring finger; referred to as the finger of the pastor, or shepherd. The ring finger becomes synonymous with caring for the needs of the flock and the heart of the church. The pastor must guard the sheep from outside and interior influences that might cause harm to those who are in his or her care. Therefore, this finger is analogous with *guard*. Lastly, there is the "little" finger, but equally important. Without the little finger the hand has no balance. This is the finger of the teacher. Without this finger, or ministry, we are lacking in a deep understanding of scripture and in their very detailed approach to things. The teacher serves to *ground* the people in the Word. Each of the fingers must do their work, because without each of the other's part there will be an incomplete hand.[7]

If the Lord has called you into one of the fivefold ministry offices, He will send confirmations as you are doing the work of the ministry. The confirmations come as you are doing, not while you're sitting. When the confirmations come, they will motivate you to continue in the work.

"And *He* gave some" (v. 11, emphasis added). The Lord is the only one who has the power to call someone into the fivefold ministry office. He is the only one with the authority to hire leaders to build His company. He does the background checks and the interviewing, hiring, and firing. He is even the one who conducts the performance evaluation to determine whether or not the person hired will receive a promotion based upon his or her work ethic and job performance.

God calls, not man. God makes the decision regarding your promotion, not man. God looks at your heart to determine your next assignment, not man. It is the Lord who pours the knowledge and wisdom into your spirit regarding your purpose, not man. Everything begins and ends with God. "I am the Alpha and the Omega, the First and the Last, the Beginning and the End" (Revelation 22:13 NIV).

"And He gave *some*." (v. 11, emphasis added). God does not call everyone into the fivefold ministry office. This doesn't mean that others are of less importance or have no responsibility within the body of Christ. All parts of the body are essential components that are needed to function as a healthy and whole body.

But now are they many members, yet but one body. And the eye cannot say unto the hand, I have no need of thee: nor again the head to the feet, I have no need of you. Nay, much more those members of the body, which seem to be more feeble, are necessary. (1 Corinthians 12:20–22)

The eye needs the hand to pick up what it sees. The head needs the feet to take it where it needs to go. We also need every hidden part of the body. We need every organ, tendon, ligament, bone, and joint in order to survive, thrive, and function. It is necessary for all members of the body to be bonded together with one another and to build each other up in love through His Son, Jesus Christ. "From him the whole body, joined and held together by every supporting ligament, grows and builds itself up in love, as each part does its work" (Ephesians 4:16 NIV). Although we are many members, having diverse functions, we are still one body.

For the body is not one member, but many. If the foot shall say, Because I am not the hand, I am not of the body; is it therefore not of the body? And if the ear shall say, Because I am not the eye, I am not of the body; is it therefore not of the body? If the whole body were an eye, where were the hearing? If the whole were hearing, where were the smelling? But now hath God set the members every one of them in the body, as it hath pleased him. And if they were all one member, where were the body? But now are they many members, yet but one body. (1 Corinthians 12:14–20)

The Lord is coming back to present unto Himself a "glorious church, not having spot, or wrinkle, or any such thing; but that it should be holy and without blemish" (Ephesians 5:27). He is coming back for His bride, a mature church that will look like Him. The apostle Paul encourages the believer to endeavor to "keep the unity of the Spirit in the bond of peace" (Ephesians 4:3). Then he goes on to remind the saints, "There is one body, and one Spirit, even as ye are called in one hope of your calling" (Ephesians 4:4). God is not coming back for a divided church but a unified church—one body.

There should be no schism in the body; but that the members should have the same care one for another. And whether one member suffer, all the members suffer with it; or one member be honoured, all the members rejoice with it. Now ye are the body of Christ, and members in particular. (1 Corinthians 12:25–27)

It is unnatural for a body to be divided against itself. If so, this points to the fact that a foreign substance may have cunningly been introduced into the body, spreading its poison throughout. In the natural, the purpose of the kidney and the liver is to flush and filter out toxins from the body. In the spirit, someone's function within the body may be to flush and filter out anything that is not like God that will try to cause dis-ease in the body of Christ. The kidney and liver are not seen outwardly, but they are major components in the life of the human body. Every organ and joint is necessary for the development and maturity of the body of Christ, "every joint supplieth" (Ephesians 4:16). Ask the Lord to reveal your role, and whatever it is, know that it is needed for the survival of the whole body.

Until we begin to see all of the fivefold ministry offices operating effectively together in the body, we will not reach the level of maturity into which God is calling the church to grow. If the leadership is divided, the rest of the body will become confused. The fivefold ministry leaders set the example. The people are watching. Not only are the people watching, but God is also watching.

Your body is a prophetic messenger. Listen to it, and make the necessary adjustments for its continued growth.

Chapter 10

PROPHETIC PROTOCOL

—•—

Let all things be done decently and in order.

—1 Corinthians 14:40

LET THERE BE

God is a God of order. In the beginning, God established order by speaking a simple and yet profound "Let!"

> In the beginning God created the heaven and the earth. And the earth was without form, and void; and darkness was upon the face of the deep. And the Spirit of God moved upon the face of the waters. And God said, Let there be light: and there was light. (Genesis 1:1–3)

If a prophet, prophetess, or one who flows in the gift of prophecy does not agree with God's established order, the *let* that is spoken out of his or her mouth is powerless and

108

will not create the form God wants established in the earth. When God made Adam, He gave him specific instructions:

> And the LORD God took the man, and put him into the garden of Eden to dress it and to keep it. And the LORD God commanded the man saying, Of every tree of the garden thou mayest freely eat: But of the tree of the knowledge of good and evil, thou shalt not eat of it: for in the day that thou eatest thereof thou shalt surely die. (Genesis 2:15–17)

God's Word provides us with the road map of how to live a godly life. If we fail to follow the instructions given to us in His Word, which is found in the Holy Bible and written under divine inspiration, we are on the road to self-destruction. Will you agree with God's instructions by obeying the protocol He has established in His Word, or will you become a prophetic puppet in the hand of the enemy?

CLOTHED IN FLESH

Giving attention to the voice of a stranger can deceive one into seeing a lie rather than hearing the truth.

> And the serpent said unto the woman, Ye shall not surely die: For God doth know that in the day ye

eat thereof, then your eyes shall be opened, and ye shall be as gods, knowing good and evil. And when the woman saw that the tree was good for food, and that it was pleasant to the eyes, and a tree to be desired to make one wise, she took of the fruit thereof, and did eat, and gave also unto her husband with her; and he did eat. (Genesis 3:4–6)

The Word of God says that the woman was "beguiled" by the serpent, which resulted in the exposure of their nakedness or sinful nature. As a result of Adam and Eve choosing to operate outside of God's divine order, God "clothed" them in "coats of skin" from an animal. "Unto Adam also and to his wife did the LORD God make coats of skins, and clothed them" (Genesis 3:21). An animal had to be sacrificed because of their disobedience. What "animal" in you has to die because of disobedience to God's instruction? Is it pride, anger, bitterness, jealousy, envy, stubbornness, lying, or gossiping? Until the animal in you dies, God's Word cannot truly resurrect through you. A prophet, prophetess, or one with the gift of prophecy who rebels against God's instruction is clothed in flesh (coats of skin) and is thereby limited to only seeing from a flaky, fleshly realm instead of from the divine, heavenly realm. A rebellious and delirious prophet or prophetess is received only by those with itching ears, those who prefer to hear falsities and fables instead of truth and theology.

> For the time will come when they will not endure sound doctrine; but after their own lusts shall they heap to themselves teachers, having itching ears; And they shall turn away their ears from the truth, and shall be turned unto fables. (2 Timothy 4:3–4)

Because of the fall of Adam and Eve, they were both expelled from the garden of Eden.

> Therefore the Lord God sent him forth from the garden of Eden, to till the ground from whence he was taken. So he drove out the man; and he placed at the east of the garden of Eden Cherubims, and a flaming sword which turned every way, to keep the way of the tree of life. (Genesis 3:23–24)

The decision to disobey the commandment of the Lord resulted in God's glory departing from man and man's removal from the garden of Eden. This resulted in man having to "till the ground" in his own strength rather than by the power of God. Adam and Eve's disobedience is rebellion in its purest form, and "rebellion is as the sin of witchcraft and stubbornness is as iniquity and idolatry" (1 Samuel 15:23).

Order from Chaos

The Spirit of the Lord does not contradict the order of God but cooperates with it. The earth responds to God's *let* and aligns the elements of nature into their proper order. As a prophet or prophetess, when your life is in proper order, and you are aligned with the will of the Father, He will cause the earth to respond to your *let*.

> "*The Spirit of the Lord does not contradict the order of God but cooperates with it.*

When God spoke *let* in the beginning, He was creating order in the chaos. As trained and seasoned prophets, our words should create order around us. This does not mean that we are to interrupt service to speak a prophetic word to the congregation because that would be out of order. It also doesn't mean that we are to give parking lot and bathroom prophecies to the people of God because that, too, is out of order. When the Lord gives us a word of prophecy for anyone in the body of Christ, it should first be shared with the pastor or the lead prophet or prophetess of the house (church). They should judge the word *before* it is delivered publically to the church body or privately to an individual. Each church's guidelines relating to prophetic flow should be sanctioned by the pastor of that church. Anyone with a prophetic word for that church should flow within those guidelines. Again, all things must be done decently and in order.

Let the Prophets Speak

The Corinthian church was rich and excelled in spiritual gifts, but there were many within the church operating in their gifts disorderly, creating confusion in the body of Christ. The apostle Paul addressed the division and disruption in the church of Corinth by starting out saying, "Now concerning spiritual gifts, brethren, I would not have you ignorant" (1 Corinthians 12:1). The Lord does not want us ignorant when it comes to spiritual gifts. You may be gifted and anointed, but there is a discipline and order involved in operating and flowing in your gift(s).

Let the prophets speak two or three, and let the other judge. If anything be revealed to another that sitteth by, let the first hold his peace. For ye may all prophesy one by one, that all may learn, and all may be comforted. And the spirits of the prophets are subject to the prophets. For God is not the author of confusion, but of peace, as in all churches of the saints. (1 Corinthians 14:29–33)

Have you ever been in a meeting where there was no written agenda passed out or provided beforehand? In that kind of meeting there is no established goal or written purpose. Many in attendance are usually talking over, above, at, or under one another. The meeting is essentially nonproductive, and many walk away frustrated. Imagine if all of the prophets, prophetesses, and those operating in the gift of prophecy were gathered in one place and all had a word from the Lord. It would be a mad circus if the word was delivered by everyone at the exact same time. This is what was going on at the church of Corinth and had to be addressed by their spiritual father, the apostle Paul.

During a church service, if the word of the Lord is given to the prophet, prophetess, or anyone with the gift of prophecy, again, the rules of the house that have been instituted by the pastor of that house must be followed. As prophetic men and women of God, we must submit to the prophetic protocol established for the house in which we are serving or attending. If you do not know the protocol, or if there is no established protocol, do not attempt to prophesy. If you prophesy suddenly during a church service, the people may leave with a lingering, unanswered question in their mind, "Was that a word from God for me?" This is because you did not hold onto that word until the appointed time of release, as determined by the protocol established for that local body.

A prophet, prophetess, or anyone with the gift of prophecy who does not wish to submit to order becomes a wandering prophetical person, walking in circles, and lost in his or her own wilderness experience. They are typically the ones who go out prematurely without the proper release from their spiritual covering. Prophetic men and women of God, your charge or release will come through your pastor by the laying on of his or her hands.

And Moses did as the LORD commanded him: and he took Joshua, and set him before Eleazar the priest, and before all the congregation. And he laid his hands upon him, and gave him a charge, as the LORD commanded by the hand of Moses. (Numbers 27:22–23)

Now there were in the church that was at Antioch certain prophets and teachers; as Barnabas, and Simeon that was called Niger, and Lucius of Cyrene, and Manaen, which had been brought up with Herod the tetrarch, and Saul. As they ministered to the Lord, and fasted, the Holy Ghost said, Separate me Barnabas and Saul for the work whereunto I have called them. And when they had fasted and prayed, and laid their hands on them, they sent them away. (Acts 13:1–3)

Jesus Christ said, "I do nothing of myself; but as my Father has taught me, I speak these things" (John 8:28). Jesus Christ, the Son of the Living God, is our greatest example of a prophet. He did not speak words from His own mind, but His words came straight from the throne room of God as He walked in alignment with His Father in heaven. As prophets and prophetesses, we are God's mouthpieces in the earth. We must be positioned at all times to see what our Father in heaven is doing and to hear what He is saying. The Word of God clearly states:

But God, who is rich in mercy, for his great love wherewith he loved us, Even when we were dead in sins, hath quickened us together with Christ (by grace ye are saved;) And hath raised us up together, and made us sit together in heavenly places in Christ Jesus. (Ephesians 2:4–6)

It is incumbent among us to speak those heavenly things that we see and hear, as we are seated "together in heavenly places in Christ Jesus."

The In-House Prophet

Bishop E. Bernard Jordan, founder of Zoe Ministries in New York, New York, makes a distinction between prophets who are out of God's order and prophets who operate in order, by coining them "out-house" and "in-house" prophets, respectively. To expand upon his distinction, out-house prophets carry a strong stench. If they prophesy in your church, the stench may linger even after they've left in the form of rebellion, sexual immorality, disunity, confusion, and all other ungodly things the out-house prophet released while he or she was there "ministering." In-house prophets, on the other hand, carry the fragrance of heaven. Their words bring life. Their thoughts are in alignment with God's thoughts; therefore, they speak the mind of Christ from the heart of God. In-house prophets submit to the under-shepherd (pastor) of the house in which they are called to minister. In-house prophets and prophetesses know how to flow in the house of God.

Are you an in-house or out-house prophet or prophetess? Do your words bring life or death? The aroma left behind will speak.

Chapter 11

PROPHETIC ASSIGNMENT

But he that knew not, and did commit things worthy of stripes, shall be beaten with few stripes. For unto whomsoever much is given, of him shall be much required: and to whom men have committed much, of him they will ask the more.

—Luke 12:48

It's a Setup

You are God's own personal investment. God has invested His time, His Word, His anointing, His Spirit, and His gifts into you for you to pour them out and into others. Again, "For unto whomsoever much is given, of him shall be much required." God has an assignment for your life, and His assignment for you speaks louder than man's annulment. Your purpose speaks louder than any pitfall or snare the enemy places before you.

God has invested His healing virtue in you by pouring Himself into you. All throughout your prophetic journey, the Lord has been setting you up. During that time of isolation, while being set apart for purpose, when you felt all alone and smothered by the dirt in your "pot of transformation," it was a setup. The Spirit of the Lord was growing you up in Him. You were set apart for a season of stretching and metamorphosis because He needed the anointing He had placed inside of you to shatter your strongholds.

Always remember, you were called out to call others in. God never forgot about you, nor did He ever forsake you. The Lord was establishing you for the work ahead. He was developing strong roots in you because of the task in front of you. He was strengthening the seed in you to break through the ground hardened by your own self-invoked limitations. He was growing you up in Him to bear much fruit. "Herein is my Father glorified, that ye bear much fruit; so shall ye be my disciples" (John 15:8).

> "God has an assignment for your life, and His assignment for you speaks louder than man's annulment.

Known by Your Fruit

Galatians 5:22–23 identifies the fruit of the Spirit: "But the fruit of the Spirit is love, joy, peace, forbearance, kindness, goodness, faithfulness, gentleness and self-control. Against such things there is no law" (NIV).

Even though your prophetic buds had begun to bloom, it was not your time to be picked to fulfill purpose. The Lord was examining the branches to see what kind of fruit it would bear. He knew the root was strong enough to bear the branches, but would the branches remain in the vine?

> I am the true vine, and my Father is the husbandman. Every branch in me that beareth not fruit he taketh away: and every branch that beareth fruit, he purgeth it, that it may bring forth more fruit. Now ye are clean through the word which I have spoken unto you. Abide in me, and I in you. As the branch cannot bear fruit of itself, except it abide in the vine; no more can ye except ye abide in me. I am the vine, ye are the branches: He that abideth in me, and I in him, the same bringeth forth much fruit: for without me ye can do nothing. (John 15:1–5)

If you do not abide in the vine, His word cannot abide in you. If God's Word does not abide in you, you may be a prophet or prophetess with *a* word but not *the* Word. As a result, you may eventually wither away, be cast into the fire, and burned. "If a man abide not in me, he is cast forth as a branch, and is withered; and men gather them, and cast them into the fire, and they are burned" (John 15:6).

Aren't you glad you stayed planted? Allow your fruit to speak for you.

> Beware of false prophets, which come to you in sheep's clothing but inwardly they are ravening wolves. Ye shall know them by their fruits. Do men gather grapes of thorns, or figs of thistles? Even so every good tree bringeth forth good fruit; but a corrupt tree bringeth forth evil fruit. A good tree cannot bring forth evil fruit, neither can a corrupt tree bring forth good fruit. Every tree that bringeth not forth good fruit is hewn down, and cast into the fire. Wherefore by their fruits ye shall know them. (Matthew 7:15–20)

The Word of the Lord says, "Ye shall know them by their fruits" (v. 16). You will not know them based upon whether or not their word comes to pass because a false prophet can give an accurate word. Balaam is a prime example of prophesying an accurate word but was later identified as a false prophet because he ventured into error. In Numbers 24:17, he prophesied the coming of the Messiah: "I shall see him, but now now: I shall behold him, but not nigh: there shall come a Star out of Jacob, and a Sceptre shall rise out of Israel, and shall smite the corners of Moab, and destroy all the children of Sheth."

However in 2 Peter 2:15–16, Balaam is identified as a prophet who had chosen the wrong path: "Which have forsaken the right way, and are gone astray, following the way of Balaam the son of Bosor, who loved the wages of unrighteousness; But was rebuked for his iniquity: the dumb ass speaking with man's voice forbad the madness of the prophet."

Balaam ventured into error by prophesying for money, prestige, fame, fortune, power, and promotion. Sexual sin, divination, witchcraft, and every evil thing awaited the fallen prophet's life and ministry. As you abide in the vine, the fruit of your labor will bear witness to others that you are one of His disciples.

ALL HAVE SINNED

We must also realize that we are yet maturing in the faith. No one is perfect but God. The Word of God reminds us that "all have sinned, and come short of the Glory of God" (Romans 3:23). There are no small or big sins; sin is sin. If we slip into sin, it will not defeat us if His Spirit lives within us. If His Spirit abides in us, we, too, will have the victory over sin and death. We must not wallow in the wilderness that we created, but repent and ask God to lead us out of that dry place. He will not just lead us out, but He will also carry us out by His Spirit if we rely totally upon His strength.

Some of us have been so broken and barren as a consequence of our sin that we can't even imagine God using us, but that is a trick of the enemy. The devil realizes that when we tap into God's strength and lift up our heads, we will see the truth of who we are in Christ Jesus. The truth is we are heirs with God and joint-heirs with Christ. The truth is we are more than conquerors through Him who loves us. The truth is we are blessed beyond measure. The truth is we cannot be plucked from His hands. The truth is God has a plan and purpose for our lives that only we can fulfill. The truth is we have been made free in Him.

The Word of God says, "He will turn again, he will have compassion upon us; he will subdue our iniquities; and thou wilt cast all their sins into the depths of the sea" (Micah 7:19). God gives all of us space to repent. The Greek word for repent is *matenoeo*, which means to change one's mind or purpose; to change one's mind for better, heartily to amend with abhorrence of one's past sins.[1] When one has truly repented of past sins, and has left them at the altar of their hearts to be consumed by God, the Lord will continue the good work He began. He will "turn again and have compassion" upon those who have truly repented, casting their sins in the "depths of the sea," never to remember them again.

Even the apostle Paul, who wrote a majority of the epistles, struggled with sin:

> For I know that in me (that is, in my flesh) dwelleth no good thing: for to will is present with me; but how to perform that which is good I find not. For the good that I would I do not: but the evil which I would not, that I do. Now if I do that I would not, it is no more I that do it, but sin that dwelleth in me. (Romans 7:18–19)

Evil is all around, but when we resist it, it will flee. We resist it by saturating our mind in the Word of God so our mind can be renewed. We resist it through prayer as the Lord speaks to us and gives us the roadmap for our prophetic journey. We resist it by associating with those of like-minds, those who will lift up our arms during our weakest moments. We resist it by not giving power to it. In other words, pay it no attention, for where your attention goes your power flows.

Even in apostle Paul's struggles he reminds us that there is "no condemnation to them which are in Christ Jesus, who walk not after the flesh, but after the Spirit" (Romans 8:1). He goes on to remind us that

[We] are not in the flesh, but in the Spirit, if so be that the Spirit of God dwell in you … But if the Spirit of him that raised up Jesus from the dead dwell in you, he that raised up Christ from the dead shall also quicken your mortal bodies by his Spirit that dwelleth in you. (Romans 8:9, 11)

The Spirit of God in you gives you the power to crucify flesh that wants to rise up through you. That same Spirit that raised Jesus is also in you and can lift you from the depths of doom and despair. The same Spirit that raised Christ from the dead can also quicken you out of your state of slumber due to sin. You are the temple of the Holy Ghost, and once you repent, forgive yourself and simply move on. However, you have the responsibility to guard your heart and to monitor that which enters your temple through all of its gates. You are the watchman on the wall of your temple. Ultimately, you are the gatekeeper guarding all entrances. "Above all else, guard your heart, for everything you do flows from it" (Proverbs 4:23 NIV).

TOTAL SURRENDER

All of the trials you have endured, the rejection you have faced, the disappointments you have encountered, and the misunderstandings you have experienced were bringing you to a place of decision in your own garden of Gethsemane where your will was surrendered into God's hands. In Gethsemane, you have reached your place of total surrender and consecration to God. "Father, if you are willing, please take this cup of suffering away from me. Yet I want your will to be done, not mine" (Luke 22:42 NLT).

You may have felt trapped in the tomb of your own theological heritage, but because of your obedience and the surrender of your will, even now the Lord is resurrecting you for the ascension and release of His gifts that were deposited in you before you were formed in your mother's womb. Yes, there was a purpose for the struggle. The Lord had to guide you through the transformation of your thoughts and the renewal of your mind so you would not see those trials and temptations as a struggle but merely steppingstones to God's greater glory being made manifest in your life. "And be not conformed to this world: but be ye transformed by the renewing of your mind, that ye may prove what is that good, and acceptable, and perfect, will of God" (Romans 12:2).

Before we can fully flow prophetically, we must be transformed into His image by the renewing of our minds. Our thoughts must become His thoughts. We must take on the mind of Christ. "Let this mind be in you, which was also in Christ Jesus: Who, being in the form of God, thought it not robbery to be equal with God" (Philippians 2:5–6).

As we submerge ourselves in His Word, our minds will become infused with His thoughts, helping us to become prophetic trailblazers in the earth and to effect the change He desires to see before His glorious return.

The Plan of Salvation

If you have not accepted Jesus Christ as your Lord and Savior in order to secure eternal life, you can do so right now. Salvation is as simple as ABC:

A: Admit to God that you are a sinner (Romans 3:23; 6:23).

B: Believe that Jesus is God's only begotten Son, and that He died on the cross for your sins, was buried, and rose again the third day (John 3:16; Acts 4:12; John 1:11–13).

C: Confess your faith in Jesus Christ as your personal Savior (Romans 10:9–11).

Now, please pray the following to be guaranteed eternal life in God:

Prayer of Salvation

Lord Jesus, I know that I'm a sinner and lost in my sins. I know I cannot save myself. Lord, I believe You came down to this earth as the Son of God, died on the cross, and rose again the third day. I believe that You did this to pay for all of my sins. I am placing my complete trust in you to save me. Right now, the best I know how, I'm asking you to please forgive my sins and save my soul. Thank you for Your free gift of salvation. In Jesus' name, Amen.

You are saved, have received the gift of everlasting life, and are eternally secure. Congratulations! Also, let me encourage you to connect with a Christian church in your area so you can further grow and develop in Christ.

Prophetic Declaration

I decree and declare that you will prophesy the Word of the Lord as the Spirit of God gives the utterance. Your words will span across prophetic air and fan into flames the spiritual gifts that have been divinely placed in God's people. I decree and declare that the words spoken from your mouth will be in sync with the heartbeat of God, in tune with the mind of Christ, and in step with His Spirit. As God leads you to prophesy in the valley, I decree and declare the dry bones will hear and obey the prophetic sound that comes forth through you. They will rise up, join together, and live!

—Prophetess Jocelyn Y. Buckley

APPENDIX
SPIRITUAL GIFTS[1, 2]

Every believer has been endowed with one or more spiritual gifts. It is important to know which gifts have been freely given to you by God. The three main Scripture passages that describe the spiritual gifts are Romans 12:6–8, 1 Corinthians 12:8–10, and 1 Corinthians 12:28–30. A brief description of each gift follows:

Prophecy—The Greek word translated "prophesying" or "prophecy" in both passages properly means to "speak forth" or declare the divine will, to interpret the purposes of God, or to make known in any way the truth of God that is designed to influence people.

Serving—Also referred to as "ministering," the Greek word *diakonian*, from which we get the English "deacon," means service of any kind, the broad application of practical help to those in need.

Teaching—This gift involves the analysis and proclamation of the Word of God, explaining the meaning, context, and application to the hearer's life. The gifted teacher is one who has the unique ability to clearly instruct and communicate knowledge, specifically the doctrines of the faith.

Encouraging—Also called "exhortation," this gift is evident in those who consistently call upon others to heed and follow God's truth, which may involve building others up by strengthening weak faith or comforting in trials.

Giving—Gifted givers are those who joyfully share what they have with others, whether financial, material, or the giving of personal time and attention. The giver is concerned for the needs of others and seeks opportunities to share goods, money and time with them as needs arise.

Leadership—The gifted leader is one who rules, presides over, or has the management of other people in the church. The word literally means "guide" and carries with it the idea of one who steers a ship. One with the gift of leadership rules with wisdom and grace and exhibits the fruit of the Spirit in his life as he leads by example.

Administration—The Greek word is *Kubernesis*. This is a unique term that refers to a shipmaster or captain. The literal meaning is "to steer," or "to rule or govern." With this gift, the Holy Spirit enables certain

Christians to organize, direct, and implement plans to lead others in various ministries of the church. It is closely related to the gift of leadership but is more goal- or task-oriented and is also more concerned with details and organization.

Mercy—Closely linked with the gift of encouragement, the gift of mercy is obvious in those who are compassionate toward others who are in distress, showing sympathy and sensitivity coupled with a desire and the resources to lessen their suffering in a kind and cheerful manner.

Word of wisdom—The fact that this gift is described as the "word" of wisdom indicates that it is one of the speaking gifts. This gift describes someone who can understand and speak forth biblical truth in such a way as to skillfully apply it to life situations with all discernment.

Word of knowledge—This is another speaking gift that involves understanding truth with an insight that only comes by revelation from God. Those with the gift of knowledge understand the deep things of God and the mysteries of His Word.

Faith—All believers possess faith in some measure because it is one of the gifts of the Spirit bestowed on all who come to Christ in faith (Galatians 5:22–23). However, the spiritual gift of faith is exhibited by one with a strong and unshakeable confidence in God, His Word, His promises, and the power of prayer to effect miracles.

Healing—This spiritual gift is closely related to the gifts of faith and miracles. All spiritual gifts are to be exercised in faith, but gifts of healing involve a special measure of it. The spiritual gift of healing is an intimate one, as it reveals the heart and compassion of God. Those who have this gift are compassionate toward the sick, have great faith, and trust that God can and will heal.

Miracles—This spiritual gift is described in Scripture much like the gift of healing. The Greek phrase *energemata dynameon* literally translates "workings of powers" involves supernatural events that can only be attributed to God. Those with the spiritual gift of miracles often have a heightened sensitivity to the presence and power of God through His Holy Spirit. They have a special measure of faith and desire for God to reveal Himself and draw many to faith in His Son Jesus Christ.

Discerning of spirits—Certain individuals possess the unique ability to determine the true message of God from that of the world; the flesh in a given situation; or that of the deceiver, Satan, whose methods include perverse, deceptive, and erroneous doctrine. The gift of discerning spirits is given to the church to protect it from such as these. It is the ability to distinguish between spirits and to discern good and evil.

Speaking in tongues—This is the spiritual gift where the Spirit enables a Christian to supernaturally speak a previously unknown language.

Interpretation of tongues—A person with the gift of interpreting tongues understands what an individual with the gift of speaking in tongues is saying even though he did not know the language that was being spoken. The tongues interpreter will then communicate the message of the tongues speaker to everyone else so all can understand.

Helps—Closely related to the gift of mercy is the gift of helps. Those with the gift of helps are those who can aid or render assistance to others in the church with compassion and grace. This has a broad range of possibilities for application. Most importantly, this is the unique ability to identify those who are struggling with doubt, fear, and other spiritual battles; to move toward those in spiritual need with a kind word and an understanding and compassionate demeanor; and to speak scriptural truth that is both convicting and loving.

Serving/Ministering—There are two Greek words for this gift. The first is *Diakonia* (Romans 12:7). The basic meaning of this word is "to wait tables," but it is most often translated as "ministry." It refers to any act of service done in genuine love for the edification of the community. The other Greek word is *Antilepsis* (1 Corinthians 12:28). It is translated "helping" (1 Corinthians 12:28). The Holy Spirit endows some believers with this gift to fill the many gaps of ministry and meet the needs of the church. They are committed to spread the gospel and serve in ways that benefit others with different gifts and ministries that are public. Those with this gift do not seek recognition or a position in the spotlight. They just love to help out.

NOTES

CHAPTER 2

1.   James Strong, *The Exhaustive Concordance of the Bible* (Nashville: Holman Bible, 1992), Hb. Word #998.

2.   "Understanding—1 Chronicles 12:32," Dr. Dan Hayden, *A Word from the Word*, accessed June 27, 2014, http://www.awordfromtheword.org/understanding

CHAPTER 3

1.   "Biblical Meaning for 'Gilgal' Eastons Bible Dictionary," Matthew George Easton, M.A., D.D., accessed June 27, 2014, http://www.bible-history.com/eastons/G/Gilgal/

2.   "Historia Religionum: Handbook for the History of Religions," C. J. Bleeker and G. Widengren, accessed June 27, 2014, http://www.en.wikipedia.org/wiki/Bethel

3. Merriam-Webster On-Line Dictionary, accessed June 27, 2014, http://www.merriam-webster.com/dictionary/valley

4. "The Law of First Mention," David L. Cooper, accessed June 29, 2014, http://www.biblicalresearch.info/page56.html

5. "Biblical Commentary on the Old Testament," Keil and Delitzsch, accessed June 28, 2014, www.biblehub.com/commentaries/2_kings/2-13.htm

6. "The Typical Meaning of the Jordan River," Roel Velema, accessed June 27, 2014, http://www.bibleone.net/print_tbs138.html

7. "Footprints in the Sand," Mary Stevenson, accessed June 27, 2014, http://www.footprints-inthe-sand.com/index.php?page=Poem/Poem.php

Chapter 4

1. "Greek Lexicon Entry For Diakonos," Thayer and Smith, accessed June 27, 2014, http://www.biblestudytools.com/lexicons/greek/nas/diakonos.html

Chapter 5

1.   The Macmillan Dictionary, accessed June 27, 2014, http://www.macmillandictionary.com/us/dictionary/american/theological

2.   "Saul— First King of Israel," Jack Zavada, accessed June 27, 2014, http://christianity.about.com/od/oldtestamentpeople/a/King-Saul.htm

Chapter 6

1.   "How Long Does It Take To Become an Expert?" Caleb Wojcik, accessed June 27, 2014, http://www.expertenough.com/2442/10000-hours-to-become-an-expert-infographic

2.   "Developing Prophetic People," Dr. Tim and Theresa Early, accessed June 27, 2014, http://65583.stablerack.com/apps/articles/default.asp?blogid=0&view=post&articleid=27554

Chapter 7

1.   The Exhaustive Concordance of the Bible, James Strong, (Nashville: Holman Bible, 1992), Hb. Word #7081

2. "Power: Baker's Evangelical Dictionary of Theology," Gary T. Meadors, accessed June 27, 2014, http://www.m.biblestudytools.com/dictionaries/bakers-evanglical-dictionary/power.html

Chapter 8

1. Merriam-Webster On-Line Dictionary, accessed June 27, 2014, http://www.merriam-webster.com/dictionary/humility

2. "Serving the Lord," William Morganfield, Sammy Stevens, and Kenneth Morris, accessed July 26, 2014, http://www.worldcat.org/title/serving-the-lord-will-pay-off-afterwhile/

Chapter 9

1. "Approaching the Heart of Prophecy: A Journey into Encouragement, Blessing, and Prophetic Gifting," Graham Cooke, (Vacaville, California: Brilliant Book House, 2006), 186

2. "The Holy Spirit and a Prophetic Culture," John Eckhardt, *God Still Speaks,* e-book, 9-11

3.   Ibid.

4.   "The Role of Prophets Today," John Eckhardt, *God Still Speaks,* e-book, 20-21

5.   Ibid.

6.   "Five- fold Ministry," accessed June 27, 2014, http://katalystchurch.org/about-us/five-fold-ministry

7.   Ibid.

CHAPTER 11

1.   "Greek Lexicon entry for Diakonos," Thayer and Smith, accessed June 27, 2014, http://www.biblestudytools.com/lexicons/greek/nas/metanoeo.html

APPENDIX

1.   "Definitions and Descriptions," accessed June 27, 2014, www.spiritualgiftstest.com/spiritual-gifts

2.   "Is there a biblical spiritual gifts list?" S. Michael Houdmann, accessed June 13, 2014, www.gotquestions.org/spiritual-gifts-list.html.

Bibliography

BibleHub.com. Accessed June 27, 2014. www.biblehub.
com/commentaries/

BibleStudyTools.com. Accessed June 7, 2014. www.
BibleStudyTools.com

Bleeker, C. J.; Widengren, G., *Historia Religionum: Handbook for the History of Religions*, Brill Academic: 1997

Cooke, Graham. *Approaching the Heart of Prophecy.* Vacaville: Brilliant Book House LLC, 2006.

Cooper, David L. "The Law of First Mention." Biblical Research Studies Group. Accessed June 29, 2014. http://www.biblicalresearch.info/page56.html

Early, Tim. "Developing Prophetic People." Identity Network. Accessed June 27, 2014. www.identitynetwork.net.

Easton, Matthew George. "Biblical Meaning for 'Gilgal.'" Bible-History.com. Accessed June 27, 2014, http://www.bible-history.com/eastons/G/Gilgal/

Easton, Mathew George. *Illustrated Bible Dictionary* (3rd Ed.). Thomas Nelson: 1897.

Eckhardt, John. "The Holy Spirit and a Prophetic Culture" and "The Role of the Prophets Today" in *God Still Speaks,* 9-11 and 20-21. Lake Mary: Charisma House, 2009, e-book

Elwell, Walter A. "Entry for 'Power." *Evangelical Dictionary of Theology*, Michigan: Baker Books, 1997

Footprints-inthe-Sand.com. Accessed June 27, 2014. http://www.footprints-inthe-sand.com/index.php?page=Poem/Poem.php

Gordon, I. "The Who Why What of Watchmen." Jesus Plus Nothing. Accessed June 27, 2014. www.jesusplusnothing.com/studies/online/Isaiah56-10-12.htm

Hayden, Dan. "Understanding – 1 Chronicles 12:32." AWordfromtheWord.org. Accessed June 2672014. www.awordfromtheword.org/understanding.

Houdmann, Michael S. "Is there a biblical spiritual gifts list?" Got Questions Ministries. Accessed June 11, 2014. www.gotquestions.org/spiritual-gifts-list.html.

Jordan, E. Bernard. *School of the Prophets Text.* Tulsa: Vincom, Inc, 1989.

"Katalyst Church A Revolution of Love." KatalystChurch. org. Accessed June 27, 2014. www.katalystchurch. org/about-us/five-fold-ministry

Keil and Delitzsch. "Biblical Commentary on the Old Testament." BibleHub.com. Accessed June 28, 2014. www.biblehub.com/commentaries/2_kings/2-13.htm

Macmillan Dictionary. Accessed June 8, 2014. www. macmillandictionary.com/us

Meadors, Gary T. "Baker's Evangelical Dictionary of Biblical Theology." BibleStudyTools.com. Accessed June 15, 2014 http://www.biblestudytools.com/dictionaries/bakers-evangelical-dictionary/power.html.

Morganfield, Willia; Stevens, Sammy; and Morris, Kenneth, *"Serving the Lord,"* Shreveport,

LA: Su-Ma Pub.; Chicago, Ill.: Exclusively distributed by Martin and Morris Music: 1971. Accessed July 26, 2014. www.worldcat.org/title/serving-the-lord-will-pay-off-afterwhile/.

SpiritualGiftsTest.com. Accessed June 27, 2014. www.spiritualgiftstest.com/spiritual-gifts

Strong, James. *Strong's Expanded Exhaustive Concordance of the Bible.* Nashville: Thomas Nelson, 2009.

Wojci, Caleb. "How Many Hours Does It Take To Become An Expert?" Expert Enough. Accessed June 27, 2014. http://www.expertenough.com/2442/10000-hours-to-become-an-expert-infographic

Zavada, Jack. "Saul— First King of Israel." About.com. Accessed June 27, 2014, http://christianity.about.com/od/oldtestamentpeople/a/King-Saul.htm

Author
Biographical Note

───── •◦• ─────

Prophetess Jocelyn Y. Buckley lives in Albuquerque, New Mexico, where she serves in ministry as an ordained elder at New Hope Full Gospel Baptist Church (FGBC), Albuquerque, New Mexico, under the pastoral leadership of Bishop David C. Cooper, senior pastor and Southwest Regional Bishop, Full Gospel Baptist Church Fellowship International (FGBCFI), and Elder Nina Cooper, co-pastor and Southwest Regional Director of Intercessory Prayer, FGBCFI. Prophetess Buckley currently serves as the director of protocol at New Hope FGBC and state director of protocol for the New Mexico, West Texas, and Colorado jurisdiction within the FGBCFI organization.

Since 1998, Prophetess Buckley has received extensive training in prophetic operations. She is recognized at her local assembly as one of the house prophets, where she has been given the authority and freedom by her pastors to prophesy as the Spirit leads. Her prophetic utterances are delivered with precision and accuracy as she fulfills God's mandate and speaks the oracles of God without compromise. In the words of her pastor and spiritual father, Bishop Cooper, "Accurate, anointed, empowered, and steeped in revelatory truth describes the ministry of Prophetess Jocelyn Buckley. Her literary insights and maturity are of one who is submitted and submerged in prophetic practical ministry."

Prophetess Buckley has earned bachelor of science degrees in mathematics (William Carey University, Hattiesburg, Mississippi) and chemical engineering (Howard University, Washington DC) and a master's degree in environmental engineering (Howard University). Prophetess Buckley earned her private pilot certificate in 2002 and became instrument rated a few years thereafter. Prophetess Buckley has accumulated over two thousand hours flying, most of which is used to fly to and from her job assignment every day.

In addition to her academic achievements, Prophetess Buckley is the first African-American woman to be inducted into the Petal High School (PHS) Academic Hall of Fame. This was indeed an honor, as Prophetess Buckley was raised in Petal, Mississippi, and graduated from Petal High School. In 2013, during the black history month festivities of the city of Petal, Prophetess Buckley was celebrated and honored for her "ongoing strive" and continuous support as well as for being an inspirational mentor to her hometown community.

Prophetess Buckley has a heart to serve and help others reach their God-given potential. In spite of her multiple achievements and accolades, she wants to be remembered as a humble, giving, and always-faithful servant.

Contact information for Prophetess Jocelyn Y. Buckley:
Email: info@jocelynbuckley.com
Web-site: www.submergedintheprophetic.com
Facebook: www.facebook.com/submergedintheprophetic
Twitter: www.twitter.com/jocelynybuckley

Printed in Great Britain
by Amazon.co.uk, Ltd.,
Marston Gate.